GOING
TO
JAIL

GOING TO JAIL

The Political Prisoner

Howard Levy, M.D. and David Miller

Grove Press, Inc.
New York

ISBN: 0–394–47584–4

Library of Congress Catalog Card Number: 76–111019

First Printing

Distributed by Random House, Inc., New York.

Manufactured in the United States of America

CONTENTS

PREFACE

I am not the same man today that I was on June 2, 1967, when I began to serve time. Twenty-six months in prison change a man.

While serving as a physician in the U.S. Army, I was outspoken in my opposition to the war in Vietnam; I refused a direct order to train Special Forces (so-called) medics. I went to jail because to have obeyed that order would have compelled me to violate canons of medical ethics which were deeply significant to me. David Miller was imprisoned for twenty-two months because he burned his draft card in opposition to the draft and the war in Vietnam. These acts were of the kind which are intensely personal. We were moral witnesses, and our acts, though not entirely without political import, were firmly rooted in individualistic soil.

Prison either breaks or nurtures political prisoners, and while most have not been broken, a few have. Some have, as Eldridge Cleaver phrases it, "become great poets or great revolutionists." David and I have not been broken nor has our poetry improved. Imprisonment freed both of us from our own egocentric prisons. Barred and locked prisons teach those who are willing to be taught that individuals acting alone cannot hope to transform a society. Acts which do not have as their aim the effective transformation of evil institutions cannot be construed as representing moral acts. My goal now is not to exhibit or defend my "pristine" moral innocence—if, in fact, it ever existed. It is to radically alter American society. To be effective in this endeavor is not *necessarily* to be moral; but to forgo an attempt at effective political action at the outset is surely immoral. These thoughts account, in part, for the detached and dispassionate tone which we have deliberately adopted for this book.

Our aim in writing this book was twofold. First, to provide a conceptual framework through which those who have never been in prison can comprehend and then challenge the prison system—a system totally lacking in socially redeeming qualities. Second, to proffer a sort of "training manual" for prospective political prisoners. Literally millions of Americans, in particular young Americans, are in revolt against the government of the United States. Many of these men and women may unfortunately be going to jail. It seems worthwhile to let them know what to expect, as well as to suggest some guidelines which might allow them to continue their revolt while incarcerated.

This book is, therefore, analytical in tone. David and I have indeed referred to our personal experiences, but only for illustrative purposes. We have alluded, occasionally angrily, to various prison administrators. It is not our intent to provide an image of these poorly misguided men as personifications of evil. They, like us, are trapped in an evil system. They have chosen to defend that system; we have elected to transform it.

We have chosen to examine the military and Federal prison systems because we can claim a certain degree of expertise concerning them. At some time or other during our prison careers we have been confined at the United States Disciplinary Barracks, Fort Leavenworth, Kansas; Allenwood Prison Farm Camp, Allenwood, Pennsylvania; and Lewisburg Federal Penitentiary and Farm Camp, Lewisburg, Pennsylvania. In addition we have drawn generously from the experiences of Donald Baty, who served time at Petersburg Federal Reformatory, Petersburg, Virginia. Also thanks to Susan Henman, whose contact with many military prisons provided valuable insight.

With this point of view it must be said that we have omitted many facets of prison life which we did not feel qualified to explore. We have not addressed ourselves to the unspeakable conditions which characterize most state penal systems. One noted civil liberties lawyer has said, concerning a client in a state prison, "the objective is to get him out alive." The overt brutality and even sadism which typify state prisons is not a prominent feature of Federal prisons. It is our belief that in the future state prisons will more and more come to resemble Federal prisons but, for the time being, the reader should not be misled; one cannot juxtapose the two systems and generalize one from the other.

The Federal prison system is America's model, but that is not saying much. Those concerned with reforming state prisons—and they are pitifully few—often wish to see the Federal system adopted. Our experience has taught us that while this may result in a superficial improvement, it will not approach the ideal: [a penal system which deters crime and rehabilitates criminals. Federal prisons do neither; furthermore, although acts of blatant physical brutality are infrequent in the Federal system, that system still cruelly dehumanizes its inmates.] Moreover, we are not convinced that physical violence will not be resorted to if Federal authorities think it required to maintain good order and discipline. The Federal government can be ruthless and may well be expected to match the state prison system's brutality blow for blow. For the time being, psychological manipulation suffices, but that should be no cause for rejoicing. If behavioral techniques fail, the whip will be cracked.

Neither have we addressed ourselves to the special problems of women prisoners and black prisoners; these people are well prepared to speak for themselves.

Finally, we have not sought to discuss the military stockade system. Although the United States Disciplinary Barracks is a military prison, unlike stockades and brigs it is modeled on the Federal system. The tens of thousands of young men incarcerated in stockades and brigs are being mistreated, abused, and, not infrequently, tortured. Approximately eighty per cent of them have committed the non-crime of being AWOL. Consciously or otherwise, going AWOL is a political act; these men, therefore, are political prisoners. Lack of detailed firsthand knowledge has compelled us to leave this area untouched.

We hope that this book will do justice to the forgotten men behind concrete walls and steel bars. Justice is their due, but for most prisoners it remains a rare commodity indeed.

—HOWARD LEVY

There are numerous memoirs and analyses of prison life in America. However, although the conditions of imprisonment are much the same for all prisoners, certain prisoners meet varying problems during their incarceration. The experience of George Jackson or Malcolm X or the four white inmates, at Indiana State Penitentiary, who wrote *An Eye for an Eye* is not our experience. Nor is it the experience of other political prisoners. We do not mean to say that we had a harder time than other prisoners; it was simply a qualitatively different kind of experience. We think that our analysis will relate best to young white Americans in terms of what a prison experience might have in store for them.

Going to Jail is not an academic, well-researched exposé of prison life. It is a biased document of opinions, anecdotes, and conclusions drawn from two years' experience in the Federal and military prison systems with the idea of quickly putting these insights into the hands of people who might face a similar experience. We feel strongly about our observations, as the reader shall see, and in fact, we would welcome a challenge to their validity provided that the inmates, the facilities, the records, and the correctional personnel of these institutions would be made entirely available to independent researchers.

There is a distinction made in the following pages between political prisoners and nonpolitical prisoners. The only purpose of this distinction is to provide the reader with a clear idea of the primary focus of the analysis. When the term "political prisoner" arises, it refers to the roughly three hundred war resisters in prison on any given day. They are the Selective-Service violators, the anti-war GIs, and the draft-file destroyers. Of course, the vast majority of inmates in American prisons are political prisoners in the wider sense of the word. Prisons reflect the class bias of the society which they serve, and the inmates are its victims: it is our continuing responsibility to point out the political nature of the courts and prisons.

Personally, I was not prepared in any real way to deal effectively with my term of imprisonment: there were reasons for this, one, certainly, having to do with my own psychology and experience. But there was more than that. I feel that I—and many other political activists—have been let down by political prisoners before us. As I recall, when speaking with friends and acquaintances who had recently served time, they either gave a superficial appraisal of prison life or they did not want to speak about it at all. I may not be entirely fair to everyone but I think that this was the general trend.

This trend is understandable but it must be overcome. The prison experience is an intensely humiliating experience; prison life is difficult to communicate to people who have not experienced "total institution" life; one would like to forget about the whole thing; if one is pressured into talking about prison, the focus will most often be on the very bad or the very good; the life style of inmates does not emerge. But if an individual is to survive the prison experience—and perhaps even make some good use of the time served—he *must* gain an appreciation of the life style of prisoners. The daily routine, the mundane details, the minor concerns, the serious problems—these are the things that Howard and I have attempted to set forth in the following pages, if only briefly.

Most of the work for the book was done at the Lewisburg farm camp while Howard and I were there together: we collaborated closely and thank the prison authorities for putting us together so that we could work to common purpose on something that neither of us probably would have set out upon alone.

—David Miller

Chapter 1 GOING TO JAIL

The prison experience begins with the laying on of hands by United States Marshals as you are led from the courtroom after your sentencing. In the event that you appealed your conviction, you are instructed to surrender yourself—after your final appeal is lost—at the U.S. Marshal's office. These men are terse and businesslike. They give you a brief shakedown, fingerprint you, and place you in a temporary lockup adjacent to their office. After spending a couple of hours in the lockup you are handcuffed and taken by car or paddy wagon to a Federal detention center to await transfer to a Federal prison. If there should be no nearby detention center you are taken instead to a county jail.

At the detention center, or county jail, the handcuffs are removed and you are told to strip. You are then given a thorough shakedown. A guard looks in your mouth, hair, armpits, under the genitals, and in the rectum. The ostensible purpose of this is to prevent the prisoner from sneaking anything into the jail and to check for venereal disease, but the process also serves to degrade and humiliate him. In most county jails underwear is returned after this shakedown and you are given a prison uniform to wear. At the Federal Detention Headquarters in New York City (the West Street jail), all clothes are taken from you except for shoes, and for the first day or two, you wear a thin bathrobe.

After you have dressed you are fingerprinted, sometimes photographed, and given a number of forms to fill out.

One of the forms is a power of attorney giving the warden, or his representatives, the right to censor all your mail. (You are requested to sign this power of attorney at all federal and military prisons. If you refuse to sign you cannot receive, or send out, mail.) The other forms deal with biographical information; name, address, occupation, educational background, previous arrest record and so on. All money and personal possessions are taken away. You may be allowed to bring a book or two into jail but, essentially, nothing else. Money and personal belongings are recorded and you are asked to sign a receipt for them.

After the in-processing is finally completed you are given sheets, blankets, a towel, shaving equipment, soap, a comb, a toothbrush, and tooth powder; then you are led to a cell. The average stay in the detention center or county jail while awaiting transfer to a Federal prison is about two weeks but can vary from one day to several weeks.

Detention centers and county jails are very dull places. There is little to do except play cards and perhaps watch television. The only decent reading material you are likely to have is that which you brought with you. Occasionally, visitors (especially clergymen) are allowed to bring you books and magazines. At Federal detention centers, visits and correspondence are usually limited to family members, clergymen, and lawyer; however, at some county jails you may correspond with and receive visits from anyone.

The usual means of transferring prisoners from detention centers to Federal prisons is by prison bus. You are handcuffed to another prisoner for the duration of the trip and there are guards at the front and rear of the bus. If you have been detained at a county jail, a marshal will escort you to the Federal prison by car. When traveling with marshals you usually wear street clothes, but on the bus you wear a prison uniform. The marshals always handcuff you, sometimes to a special belt or chain draped around the waist.

In general, during the process which we have thus far described, the marshals and prison guards will not do you any physical harm. But if you engage in any acts of non-cooperation (such as refusing to walk, or to submit to fingerprinting) you might be assaulted.

If your destination is some distance from the point at which you began your imprisonment you may have to stop over at a number of county jails and/or Federal prisons en route. The stopover time varies from one night to several weeks.

Upon arrival at your final destination you are led through the front gate of the prison and are taken to the receiving-and-discharge section of the prison and told to strip so that prison personnel can once again give you another thorough shakedown. You then shower and are issued a clean prison uniform, after which you are again fingerprinted, photographed, and given a myriad of forms to fill out. All your clothes, including your shoes, and personal possessions that you are not allowed to bring into the institution are put in a package to be sent to your home; any money you may have is placed in your commissary account. Finally, you are given a shave, a haircut (at some, but by no means all Federal institutions all your hair is shaved off upon arrival), and a number.

Your first couple of weeks in the institution are spent in a special "admission and orientation" section (A&O). During this period you are given a complete physical examination, including blood and urine tests, a chest X ray, and various inoculations. You take a battery of aptitude and mental tests and attend a number of lectures. These are mundane and deal with such subjects as safety, health, education, and other aspects of prison life. You are advised to ask the prison staff about anything concerning prison procedure, but the fact is that the staff usually tells you very little, and the new prisoner ends up learning the rules and routines from other inmates.

Prisoners who have been assigned to minimum-security camps usually spend a few days behind the walls of the penitentiary before being transferred. For example, inmates en route to Allenwood Farm Camp spend about a week in the A & O section of Lewisburg Federal Penitentiary, while those who are destined for the Lewisburg Penitentiary Farm Camp often spend a month or two in the population at the penitentiary before they are moved out to the farm camp. In either case you can expect to spend a minimum of one or two weeks in the A & O section before you have completed processing; at which time you will be given a job assignment and permanent quarters. After that, you are ready to begin doing time in earnest.

CLASSIFICATION

There are three categories of security classification: maximum, medium, and minimum. Almost, but not quite without exception, political prisoners are classified minimum security. The one major exception is in military prisons, where political prisoners are classified either maximum- or medium-security; but even within the military, a few achieve the status of minimum-security prisoners.

Maximum- and most medium-security prisoners are never allowed outside the penitentiary except to be transported to court; purportedly, the risk of escape is the greatest with maximum-security inmates. For instance, at Lewisburg, the industry building must be approached by crossing the prison yard. On occasion, there are fogs, and some men have to remain inside without going to work because they are not "cleared for fog." Apparently, the worry is that they would take the opportunity to storm the thirty-foot-high wall.

Minimum-security prisoners populate the farm camps. They are, in a sense, honor prisoners because it is considered that they will not run away. At the minimum-security camps there are no high walls, barbed-wire fences, locked doors, barred windows, or armed guards. Supervision on and off the job is at a minimum and the opportunity for escape is ever present. Medium-security prisoners form a "limbo" category—supposedly between the best and worst risks. They are afforded greater freedom of movement within the penitentiary and a few may be permitted to perform work outside the prison walls, albeit under the constant supervision of prison personnel.

In theory, prisoners progress from maximum, through medium, to minimum security and this progression represents a measure of the prisoner's capacity for rehabilitation. Political prisoners do not fit into this scheme because they are almost invariably classified minimum security. But even if we are to exclude political prisoners as a special case, the theory is faulty.

There are a large number of men behind the walls who could just as easily fit into the prison camps as that minority of prisoners actually assigned there. On the other hand, there are men in the prison camps who, by general prison standards, should not be there. The explanation for these inconsistencies relates to the twofold purpose of the farm camps. Firstly, the farm camps are useful to the prison establishment because they serve to illustrate the progressive nature of Federal prisons. They are thus, in part, a propaganda tool. Secondly, and probably the determining factor for the existence of the farm camps, a certain number of men are needed to perform work outside the walled-in area of the penitentiary itself. Most of the groundwork, farm work, and garage maintenance that support the institution, as well as the upkeep of the prison reservation is done by the minimum-security inmates. Conversely, there are men who want and supposedly deserve minimum-security rating, but are denied access to the farm camps because they possess a job skill that is needed within the penitentiary. Thus, skilled draftsmen who may be serving a year or two for a marijuana bust, and who have had no previous criminal record, are not sent to the farm because their talents can be put to better advantage in one of the industrial shops within the penitentiary.

At the other extreme, prisoners who by no criteria should be sent to the farm camp, sometimes are so assigned because they, too, possess a skill which can be put to best advantage on the farm. To take a ludicrous but true example, Allenwood Farm Camp, extremely proud of its fine softball team, was assigned superlative softball players regardless of whether or not they met the standard for placement at that camp.

There is, of course, no such thing as a permanent classification. The warden giveth and the warden may taketh away. Hence, inmates who violate the rules of the institution often find themselves reduced from minimum security, along with the attendant loss of privileges which that implies.

One of the authors [H.L.] was changed from medium- to maximum-security classification while at the Disciplinary Barracks, Fort Leavenworth, for his "failure to properly make his dust cover." (A dust cover is a blanket which is to be placed over the pillow during the daytime hours.) The other [D.M.] was changed to maximum custody for protesting "make-work" at Allenwood Farm Camp (*see* "Resistance").

Since prisoners highly value their minimum-security classification, this threat of reassignment of classification status is used effectively by the prison administration as part of its arsenal of manipulative rewards and punishments.

QUARTERS

A prisoner's living quarters are called his domicile area. At the USDB most prisoners lived in two- or four-man cells. A minority of prisoners lived in a dormitory setting. In Federal prisons most prisoners live in a dormitory setting. A typical dormitory consists of one large room containing double bunk beds and housing upward of fifty men.

All Federal prisons also contain cells, and many seasoned veterans of the prison system prefer a one-man cell to a dormitory. The one-man cells, however, are not numerous enough to go around, and most men consequently are forced to reside in a dormitory. The advantage of a one-man cell is the degree of quiet and privacy invariably lacking in a dormitory. For the man doing a generous stint, the opportunity to masturbate in the solitude of his own cell is a highly valued privilege.

At the farm camps there are no cells. Prisoners live either in a dormitory or in small rooms, each shared by four or five men. A typical room measures approximately ten by fifteen feet.

Prison officials have carefully and knowingly constructed their prisons so that the housing arrangements can be utilized as yet another manipulatory tool. Prisoners are rewarded for good behavior by being provided with improved domicile privileges. At Lewisburg Federal Penitentiary most prisoners were sent from A & O to the "F" wing of the prison; "F" wing was known as the "jungle." It was also understood by prisoners and prison officials alike that "F" also meant "fuck." In the jungle men could expect to be subjected to homosexual advances. In fact, prisoners are not infrequently raped in "F" wing.

Prison officials at Lewisburg were assiduous in assigning not all but a select few political prisoners to "F" wing. This was done because they felt that the intimidation of a few political prisoners would suffice to keep all political prisoners in line as the word spread around.

In any event, living quarters, like almost everything else in prison, fit into a complicated jigsaw puzzle which can be fully understood only when it is realized that prisoner manipulation is the intent and practice of the authorities.

HAIRCUTS, SHAVES, AND GENERAL DEPORTMENT

Personal grooming should be just that, personal. This is not so, though, in prison. The grooming standard is set and maintained with little leeway given by the staff. The standard is a clean-shaven face, closely cropped hair, and polished shoes. The standard, it must be said, is less severe in Federal prisons than it is in their military counterparts.

If a man has a slight growth of beard or if his sideburns seem to be creeping down his face, he will be told by any number of hacks (i.e., guards), "bring me a shave [or haircut] tomorrow." Visiting time is when the prisoner most frequently gets caught. The threat of not allowing one to see a visitor unless he meets the strict standards is a most effective means of securing the prisoner's compliance. If the prisoner refuses to comply, additional hardships and punishments will surely be imposed. Often it is a game to see how far one can go before getting caught. Some prisoners express their disgust with the haircut rules by shaving their heads completely bald. It is sometimes difficult to be sure whether their protest is conscious or not; however, the practice is more common than might be supposed. It is one of innumerable examples of tacit prison resistance.

In some long past era rules governing haircuts and shaves made a great deal of sense. Prisons, together with military camps, were, because of overcrowding and inadequate sanitation, breeding grounds for lice, scabies, and bacterial infection. Hence, the insistence upon a clean face and short hair was a matter of hygiene, and not a question of standardization. One would therefore be tempted to suppose that present-day standards are nothing more than a remaining vestige of past standards—sensible enough then, but outmoded and antiquated today. But this generous interpretation is weakened when we are forced to consider other, less easily explicable rules governing personal appearances.

There are rules that govern things like tucking the shirt inside the pants, wearing a sweat shirt as an outer garment in the dining hall, and the type of footwear permitted in the dining hall (boots and shoes are in, slippers are out). The reformatory, correctional institution, and the military prison are likely to give the prisoner more of a hassle in these areas than will the penitentiary. As one inmate put it, the former "try to reform you by harassing the shit out of you."

One of the authors [H.L.] was threatened with solitary confinement while at the USDB because his sideburns were, by prison officials' statements, "one-eighth of an inch too long." Needless to say, he trimmed them to size upon the request of the officials.

Taken as a whole, one is led to consider the standards of personal grooming as a reflection of the para-military operative modes of most penal institutions, as well as a mirror image of the bourgeois standards of prison personnel. The man who may have murdered twenty children but who wears a crewcut is far more likely to find social acceptance among the ranks of prison personnel than the young, long-haired man convicted of possession of marijuana.

Personal hygiene, as opposed to personal grooming, is left to the individual. Prison officials prefer well-scrubbed, clean inmates, but since non-compliance with this standard is less visible than a luxuriant head of hair, harassment at the hands of prison officials is less of a problem. Showers are up to the inmate; but if an inmate is overly remiss here, social pressure from his peers will quickly enough change his habits. All prisons are overcrowded and, personal preferences notwithstanding, the stench of fifty unbathed men in a dormitory could be somewhat overwhelming.

A related area of concern is the cleanliness of one's "house." Privacy does not exist in prison and the closest approximation to it is the domicile area. It is to your room, or dormitory section, or cell that you must retreat when you wish to escape from the prison crowd; it is your sanctuary. Unfortunately, it is not yours alone and most often must be shared with other inmates. Your roommates will, in all probability, demand that the room be kept spotless. They will expect you to pull your weight in sweeping, mopping, and buff-waxing the floor. In addition, the windows will have to be cleaned, ash trays and waste cans emptied. Prison officials make periodic inspections to keep everyone on his toes. In the military prison these inspections are taken quite seriously, and disciplinary reports may be made on inmates whose rooms are not up to par.

One of the authors [H.L.] was put on at least a half-dozen disciplinary reports for failure to maintain the cleanliness of his area during the course of thirteen months at the USDB. By contrast, at Lewisburg Farm Camp, he experienced no difficulty in this regard. In Federal prisons, such discipline is less common, in part because the discipline is already present and is enforced by the inmates themselves. In larger part, the difference probably has more to do with the greater degree of maturity of both inmates and prison personnel in Federal prisons.

Political prisoners tend to be a nonconformist lot when it comes to matters of personal grooming and hygiene. They tend to place far less emphasis upon these social customs than do their fellow inmates. For the most part, however, political prisoners have experienced no great difficulty in adjusting to the demands which both prison officials and prisoners make in this regard. It is our opinion that it is far easier to go along with the mores of the prison population and officials, even though at times their obsessive cleanliness and neatness is exasperating. The alternative is to do your thing; however, in our experience, those few political prisoners who have done so were soon totally isolated and ostracized from the rest of the prison community.

HOURS AND COUNTS

Twenty-four hours a day, seven days a week, the hands of the clock determine where you are and what you should be doing; the meaning of a total institution is painfully clear. "I have measured out my life in coffee spoons," says the poet. Regimentation and routine are parceled out in hours and minutes. With a small variance that itself becomes institutionalized, meals, work, recreation, education, and sleep are kindly scheduled for your benefit, and sandwiched in are the dehumanizing body counts.

The entire institution is counted at 12:00 midnight, 3:00 A.M., 5:30 A.M., 4:30 P.M. and 10:00 P.M. At the farm camps a noon count is added. Each man has to be in a specific place for each count, and from midnight to 5:30 A.M. all inmates are expected to be in their respective bunks.

Count must be "cleared" before activity can begin again. If the count is "off" (i.e., incorrect), it is taken again. If it is off again, a bed check is ordered. This means that all prisoners must go to their beds, where they can be more easily counted. If it is ultimately determined that an inmate is, in fact, missing, it has to be determined who that inmate is before the count can be O.K.'d and the general routine resumed.

"Fucking up the count" is frowned upon by staff and usually by inmates as well. Disciplinary action will be taken if a man fails to report or reports late to the area in which he is to be counted. For the guards, obtaining a correct count seems, at times, to represent their only job fulfillment. They seem to feel that incorrect counts are injurious to their reputation, and since their superiors are present when counts are taken this may, indeed, be true. When the count is "fucked up," inmates become irritated because they much prefer to get on with their business instead of standing in one place while the count is repeated, and there are choice comments for hacks who cannot seem to count. Of course, "fucking up the count" by escaping is readily forgiven by inmates.

FOOD

The food in Federal joints (i.e., prisons) is usually compared favorably to that of state or county jails. Some prison connoisseurs say it even compares favorably with institutional food in general, for instance, that of schools and hospitals. It is, except for beef, plentiful.

However, prison diets, like those of other institutions, are deficient in that individual palates cannot be provided for. The food, its method of preparation, and the amount received is out of the control of the recipient. A prisoner goes through the food line and takes his choice of what is available. While he may heap up the potatoes and gravy, the vegetables and the bread, the choice items are guarded. Under the watchful eye of a hack, an inmate food-service worker serves one piece of meat and one portion of dessert to each man. The food is almost always overcooked and unimaginatively spiced; steaming is a favorite kitchen device; and potatoes and canned vegetables are steamed again as they sit in their containers in the steam table.

One might facetiously say that the menu for each meal is a gas, but the humor fades with exposure. Prisoners are treated to potatoes—snowflake potatoes, steamed or boiled potatoes, hot, buttered potatoes, and shoestring potatoes. During any particular week, hamburger patties, meat loaf, Salisbury steak, and Swedish meat balls might be served, only the names and shapes changing in each instance.

Breakfast for the main population begins at 6:30 A.M. Prior to that the food-service inmates have arisen, prepared breakfast, and eaten. Bacon and eggs appear once or twice a week at Federal prisons—two slices of bacon and two eggs. Dry cereal and a bowl of whole milk, with possible seconds of milk, are served every day. Alternatively, there are hot cakes, French toast, chipped beef on toast (also known in the military as "shit on a shingle"), steamed oatmeal, and so on. Breakfast is over by 7:30 A.M.

At 10:20 A.M. "short line" lunch begins. This is the lunch

meal for the food-service workers and a few other inmates who have specialized jobs. The main population feeds from 11:30 to 12:30. They are called to the dining room in groups as they are let off their work details. Lunch is over by 1:00 P.M. At the farm camps, where the population is much smaller, all prisoners eat at more or less the same time.

At 3:20 P.M. "short line" supper begins. Again, this is primarily for the food-service workers. At about 4:30 P.M., supper starts for the main population. Inmates are called by dormitories or groups of dormitories on a rotation schedule which changes from day to day. One group eats first one evening, another group eats first the next evening, and so on. Again, at the farm camps all inmates eat at the same time. By 6:00 P.M. supper has ended.

The prison community produces some of the food it consumes. The Allenwood camp, for example, provides most of the beef for itself and Lewisburg from the thousand head of Herefords raised there. At the Lewisburg Farm Camp, the dairy produces the milk and the piggery the pork. This is a pattern generally followed around the country—the farm camps attached to and providing food for the parent institution.

At first glance it is paradoxical that an institution like the United States Disciplinary Barracks, which has only a token farm camp is able, by and large, to provide better food for its inmates than Federal prisons that possess larger farms. However, it is easily enough explained. The Federal penal system relies upon the farm camps as a way of reducing the prices it must pay for food; the variety and quality of inmate food needs are secondary considerations. On the other hand, an institution like the USDB, which cannot rely upon its own farm for food supplies, is able to provide an adequate yearly budget which is expended to purchase high-quality beef, chickens, eggs, milk, and fresh vegetables. The Associate Warden of Lewisburg once admitted that were Lewisburg Farm Camp abolished, the inmates would undoubtedly receive better food.

It is against the rules for a prisoner to take food out of the dining room. This rule is followed more closely in the penitentiary than at the minimum-security camps. Food-service personnel are often shaken down before leaving work in order to cut down on pilfering. Pieces of cake, cookies, or meat sandwiches do make it back to the dormitories though. If an old-timer sees a newcomer making a sandwich for the evening, he might comment that the man was really "learning how to jail." It is, of course, also against the rules for the kitchen stewards, employees of the prison, to steal food from the mess hall. But it is widely suspected, and at times confirmed, that prison personnel do pilfer food, especially the better cuts of beef. This practice naturally results in the diminished availability of beef which, under the best of circumstances, is in scarce supply.

Despite the fact that the food at some prisons may be better than at others it is still true that institution food is institution food. The knowledge that people are starving all over the world cannot alter the oppressive regularity of the same basic menu eaten at the same time at the same place seven days a week with no change except for the inmate voluntarily to miss a meal. The atmosphere cannot be described as cozy. The dining room holds several hundred men with all the ensuing noise; voices, banging trays, and crashing silverware. The farm camps have plastic plates and sometimes real china, but behind the wall, there are only metal trays to eat from. Unless you happen to be first in line—and the overcrowded conditions make all the lines long—it is "eat and run" well within a half-hour

There is too little time for the dining hall to be a gathering place, yet it is, indeed, a highly social setting. With *whom* you eat is a very significant interpersonal and intergroup act. Almost more than anything else, your eating companions define you in the eyes of the other inmates. There are variants, of course, but social status and social groups are set in this way, and set rather quickly too.

Eating as a part of prison life must be considered a primary diversion and time-consumer. An inmate's eating habits are developed more from routine than necessity. After a time a pattern of stimulus and response emerges that has very little to do with bodily needs: you eat because it is time to eat, everyone else is eating, and it is one of the breaks in a strictly regimented environment. The pattern is hard to avoid. Some prisoners experiment with their eating habits and preferences, partly in order to express their individuality while confined. For example, prisoners will learn the alleged benefits of vegetarianism; other prisoners, in particular blacks, will eschew pork. In part, these voluntary restrictions are based upon religious motivations; however, it is difficult to escape the conclusion that they also represent attempts to retain some sense of personal uniqueness.

Food, like nearly everything else in prison, is used by the prison authorities to promote a healthy façade for public consumption. During visiting hours, for example, visitors are permitted to order lunch for themselves. Ordinarily, their lunch is identical to that of the inmate population.* However, when an especially poor meal is being served in the dining room, visitors will be served better fare, usually prepared the day before. Then too, visitors, unlike inmates, are supplied paper napkins and they eat

---

* There are no meals served to visitors at the USDB.

off plates, not metal trays; they are served coffee in china cups, not metal bowls or plastic cups. All of this is intended to impress visitors with the conviviality of the Federal Bureau of Prisons. It is wise to tip visitors off as to the true state of affairs.

Another public-relations ploy has to do with the connection between the quality of meals and the availability of foodstuffs at the prison commissary. We have detected an inverse relationship between the adequacy of the diet and commissary privileges. Where the food is better, the amount of money allowed for commissary and the variety of goods offered is less. The Federal Bureau of Prisons obviously feels that if abundant foodstuffs are available in commissary, the public might be led to the conclusion that such availability is an indication that the Bureau is inadequately feeding its prisoners. As a result, only snacks are available at commissaries in Federal prisons, whereas in state prisons canned food, sandwiches, and soup can also be purchased.

CLOTHING

Prison blues and prison khaki are both in use throughout the Federal system. At the USDB, seal browns, that is, old, green, Army fatigues dyed brown are what the well-dressed military prisoner is wearing. Most of the Federal prisons are, however, switching over to khakis and the remaining stocks of blues are being phased out.

Every inmate, on being received into any Federal penitentiary or prison camp is issued about four sets of clothing. The underwear, pants, and shirts are stamped with a number which corresponds with the inmate's own laundry-bin number. After the dirty apparel has made its way through the prison laundry, it is separated by number and placed in the proper bin to await the clothing pickup. Clothing exchange varies somewhat from institution to institution. A typical clothing-exchange schedule runs something like this: kitchen and hospital whites, underwear, and towels on Tuesday; sheets and pillowcases on Wednesday; blues and socks on Friday. On certain nights a special line is arranged for those who wish to complain of a shortage, i.e., clothing turned in but never given back.

There never seem to be enough good shoes available. Sweaters, coats, boots, and other outdoor apparel are usually in short supply. In these categories the best go first, often to those inmates who work in clothing issue, and their friends. As far as getting the best available, working in clothing issue is a strategic position.

Athletic clothing must be purchased through the commissary. This apparel is a near necessity if one is to get a reasonable amount of physical exercise, since the regular clothing is inappropriate. One is able to purchase sweat shirts, sweat pants, sweat socks, and sneakers, as well as "luxury" items such as handballs and baseball gloves.

The uniformity and conformity of the clothing is a significant element in the blandness and drabness of prison life. As bad as clothing fads on the outside may be, they are to be preferred to prison fashion. In our culture, men and women distinguish themselves, in part, by the clothes they choose to wear. There is an attempt on the part of prisoners to do likewise; however, the limited variety of apparel available makes the attempt sometimes look ludicrous. Thus the Black Muslims can be distinguished from other prisoners by the fact that they invariably button the top buttons of their shirts. Other prisoners may elect to wear a distinguishing cap and at times, wear it inside the dormitory. Still others use India ink to paint words and pictures on their sweat shirts. There are innumerable variations on these themes, and while they often seem trivial they should not be casually dismissed: they represent aborted attempts at asserting one's individuality. As prison officials insist upon homogeneity, the men being so treated insist on being recognized as individuals. Each one knows that he, though a prisoner like every other prisoner, is still a man, a bit different and distinct from every other man. Subverting one's prison uniform is at once a significant and pathetic attempt to retain this birthright.

Nor should the political significance of these small acts of defiance be overlooked. The black inmate who wears a sweat shirt upon which he has drawn a clenched fist is making an important political statement. And the USDB anti-war GI's would often use a pointed shop tool to etch a peace symbol on their metal belt buckles. The message is at once hackneyed and profound: "You've got my body, but not my mind."

Chapter 2 COMMISSARY

The institution provides all of the inmates' basic needs. But for those inmates, and they are the majority, who feel the need for such amenities as pens, cigarettes, cigars, pipe tobacco, cookies, candy, toilet articles, and the like, there is a commissary available.

At most Federal institutions, inmates are permitted to spend twenty dollars a month. Any money which the prisoner may have had in his possession when he arrived at the prison will be placed in his commissary fund. Visitors may leave money for the fund or are permitted to send it to the inmate through the mail. (Money orders are preferable because they can be expeditiously handled.) At the USDB, inmates can purchase only six dollars' worth of goods each month; the selection is more limited and prices very much cheaper than at Federal prisons. Unlike Federal prisoners, USDB inmates are credited with the six dollars each month and do not spend their own money. In no prison are inmates permitted to handle money directly. As a substitute, cigarettes and other items are frequently used as barter.

At most institutions, inmates are permitted to go to commissary once a week; at the USDB, commissary privilege is available only once a month. In most Federal prisons athletic equipment, including sweat shirts, sweat pants, sneakers, and other paraphernalia is also available, and often can be purchased from funds outside of the twenty-dollar limit.

Most prisoners, despite the always present, long, slow-moving lines, eagerly look forward to their commissary days. The goods available, limited as they are, provide a break in the monotony of the daily prison fare, and the snack items, including coffee, hot chocolate, and tea (all unavailable at the USDB) help to fill in the long hungry hours between early dinner and the next morning's breakfast. But, as is true of most other prison privileges, commissary is not entirely without its shortcomings and drawbacks.

In Federal prisons, the fact that inmates must spend their own money imposes a hardship upon the poorer prisoners. The unavailability of commissary funds for poor prisoners contributes to prison gambling. Then, too, some prisoners may ask others to buy goods for them. This may be all right if done occasionally; however, this kind of arrangement can degenerate into a dependent relationship which may later have pernicious effects upon affairs unrelated to commissary. Most political prisoners are exceedingly generous with the goods which they have bought for themselves and this, to some extent, might be preferable to the outright purchase of goods for other prisoners.

In some institutions, most notably reformatories, inmates will steal items from one's locker and at times even from one's person as he is leaving the commissary line. But stealing occurs quite infrequently in adult prisons and farm camps, certainly never in the open. There is a fairly sophisticated honor system about stealing from lockers. No one in prison likes a jail-house thief, especially not the type who steals nickel-and-dime commissary items. We knew one political prisoner who had a couple of cartons of cigarettes stolen from his locker at a farm camp. It was obvious that they were taken by a man who simply was a compulsive gambler, up to his ears in debt. Several men got together, without any encouragement from the political prisoner, caught the culprit, and gave him a few light raps on the nose. The inmates, who by then had won the cigarettes from the thief in a poker game, tried to give them back to the political prisoner.

For those men who feel especially paranoid about jail-house thieves, combination locks can be purchased for personal lockers. Few, if any, political prisoners have had the need to do so, and up until now theft in adult prisons has been an insignificant problem.

In light of the disadvantages of commissary, a few political prisoners feel that it is best to avoid the commissary altogether. Of course, this alternative does not so much solve the problems as evade them. For the most part, political prisoners, along with the general inmate population, utilize their commissary privileges and do their best with whatever problems may arise.

Chapter 3 CONTRABAND

Contraband may be defined as any article introduced into or manufactured on the premises of a Federal or military prison which is not explicitly approved of by the authorities of that institution. But given the mazelike corpus of prison regulations this simple definition does not quite suffice. An article that is permissible in one place may be contraband a few hundred feet away. For example, a prisoner who has received permission from the Education Department to possess a given book may have that book in his domicile area; however, were he to carry it to his work area it might be deemed contraband.

Every prisoner possesses contraband. Prison life, always difficult, would be intolerable were it not for the comforts which contraband secures. The most common articles of contraband include unapproved books and periodicals, food which is removed from the mess hall, and extra articles of clothing. But at any given time one may find prisoners who possess almost any conceivable contraband. In the bland environment of prison, personal belongings, themselves often scarcely worthy of note, loom large in importance. To say that such and such a knickknack is a personal item is at once to affirm one's identity and to preserve one's self in the context of a de-individualizing and depersonalizing prison society.

Aside from the sheer personal pleasure which accrues from the possession of contraband, the latter also serves very real utilitarian functions. For some prisoners, defensive weapons, such as knives, are a necessity; for political prisoners books, periodicals, extra pens and pencils, stamps, plain envelopes, carbon paper, and so forth are the normal objects of trade; and for all prisoners contraband food relieves the long hours between dinner and breakfast, while clothing, that is, clothing above and beyond the regular issue, affords needed comfort, especially in colder climates.

In general, prison officials are lax in enforcing the regulations pertaining to contraband. The officials are doubtless aware of the extent of this particular breach of prison rules, but have obviously adopted a desultory policy. The reason may simply be a matter of practicality, for if authorities were to crack down on those inmates who possess contraband it would be necessary to construct an entirely new prison to house all the offenders. On the other hand, prison officials are not completely oblivious to the problem. Shakedowns, either of individual prisoners or entire domicile areas, do occur. And prisoners leaving the mess hall are frequently frisked.

Shakedowns, however, are not calculated to search out all contraband material but, rather, specific items, such as weapons. Then, too, certain inmate employees are regularly subjected to shakedowns; kitchen workers, for example, are invariably frisked as they leave the kitchen. In this case, the authorities are not only on the lookout for weapons but for yeast. The latter is a closely guarded commodity since it is a prime ingredient used in the manufacture of "home brew." Even at institutions such as the USDB, where officials are shakedown-addicted, the yield in terms of seizure of contraband is likely to be minimal. The greater the surveillance, the greater the diligence and ingenuity with which prisoners hide their cache. Sometimes the most obvious hiding places do the trick. At the USDB, one of the authors [H.L.] "hid" an incriminating manuscript on a clipboard which was hanging, quite prominently, on the wall of the photography shop in which he worked. A half-dozen shakedowns succeeded only in exposing, and hence destroying, hundreds of dollars worth of film; the manuscript was never discovered. Shakedowns sometimes become ritualistic habits for prison authorities but are conducted halfheartedly. At the USDB, repeated shakedowns failed to reduce the availability of marijuana, and indeed, this drug was far more readily accessible at the USDB than it was at Lewisburg Federal Penitentiary where shakedowns were less frequent.

Hiding places for contraband are innumerable but are best left undiscussed; the same goes for methods of getting contraband material to and from prisoners. One quickly enough becomes acquainted with these techniques soon after arrival in prison. For now, we can only marvel at the dedicated experimentation, trial and error, and genuine inventiveness which multitudes of prisoners have exhibited in perfecting these techniques. One example is worthy of note.

We were acquainted with a prisoner who had been confined to the hole for an extended period of time. He was not permitted to have cigarettes but everyone in the prison, guards and officials included, knew that the young man was smoking daily; yet dozens of shakedowns failed to reveal his cache. What the inmate had done was to cut a well—in which he hid the cigarettes—in the only book he was permitted to possess: the Bible. While not exacly in the Willie Sutton league, we feel that any man able to use the Good Book in this way is deserving of honorable mention.

Though it is true that punishment for the possession of contraband is relatively infrequent, it should be stressed that occasionally men are sent to the hole and "good time" is taken away for this infraction. This is most likely to occur when the contraband in question, from the point of view of prison officials, is of an especially odious nature. Such articles might include weapons, narcotics, needles, glue (glue-sniffing is a favorite pastime at reformatories), and pornographic material; in the case of possession of clearly illegal goods, such as narcotics and marijuana, criminal prosecution may very well ensue; the possession of "home brew" is an intermediate case. In some institutions this wholesome beverage is regularly confiscated, but punishment rarely results. At Allenwood prison farm, five or six guards would regularly sweep down upon a targeted domicile area, blockade the exits, and tear the inmates' lockers apart. An eyewitness to one such raid remarked that it must have been staged and directed by Elliot Ness; but it was all mostly a matter of role-playing, since the booty was merely confiscated. The offender was not so much as reprimanded. Political prisoners have been known to sip "home brew" and on occasion to have even taken a few drags on a weed.

We do not recommend that political prisoners forgo the benefits of their educational tools; for them to do so would be to sever their life line to the outside world. We do, however, recommend that they use and distribute these materials with care and discretion. It is not advisable to place one's name on contraband books; it is better to lose the book than to be busted for its possession and/or illegal transfer to another inmate. It is best to remove mailing labels from all publications soon after they reach you. If these publications are later confiscated, only the possessor will be busted, and, what is more crucial—since these publications are widely distributed—the possessor may not be the owner. Therefore, the point of origin of the publication cannot be discovered unless, of course, prison officials carefully review all incoming periodicals. The latter, though an awesome and time-consuming task, is sometimes resorted to. However, such intensive surveillance, as opposed to the routine screening usually employed, often breaks down in a few weeks; moreover, much of this material does not enter prison through normal mail channels anyway. If, despite due precautions, you should be apprehended with contraband material of any kind, never allow your inquisitors to know the person from whom you received the material, or the way in which the material entered prison.

The care which you will be forced to use in hiding political contraband will vary with the degree of anxiety of particular prison officials. At the USDB, where Army officials felt that a Communist was lurking in every corner, inmate security was a requirement, whereas at Lewisburg farm camp, no political literature was censored. As a consequence, and by definition, political prisoners did not "harbor" this type of "contraband." One ventures to suggest that so simple a solution might recommend itself to all prison administrations, but the sad truth is that such is not yet the case.

As with any other prison regulation, punishment for its violation often depends upon the personal whim or fancy of a particular guard or official. We believe that our previous statement that prison officials are, by and large—with the already noted exceptions borne in mind—unconcerned about contraband, holds true. But this is not to say that individual prison personnel, in particular guards, are not ready to "bust ass" over the matter of contraband. The "ball busters" are well-known to the prison population and when they are on duty extra care is much in evidence.

Although we are unaware of it happening, it is not far-fetched to assume that prison officials may, on occasion, use the violation of the rules pertaining to contraband as a means to punish and segregate political prisoners, much as marijuana busts may be used to silence campus radicals. Conceivably, were one able to prove a pattern or practice of selective discrimination concerning political prisoners, legal assistance might be sought. But Federal courts have, for the most part, adopted a "hands off" doctrine when it comes to so-called "administrative" decisions of prison officials. Furthermore, an allegation of selective punishment of a political prisoner might be well-nigh impossible to prove; for these reasons we are most pessimistic that one can find relief in the courts. But, as is often the case, the mere threat of legal action sometimes results in a curtailment of discriminatory practices. Much the same holds true if one is able to expose the situation publicly.

(The following addendum is by David Miller.)

I was no exception in the need for contraband to make life a little more pleasant. For the twelve months that a roommate of mine said that I had a cereal "Jones" (a habit), I possessed a bowl and spoon that I had lifted from the dining hall; I kept them in my locker. At breakfast I would steal a few of the individual-portion boxes of cereal put out. Cheerios and Wheaties were my favorites, but if all they had were Rice Toasties, they had to do. I also stole sugar, which I placed in an empty cereal box. I did not learn the best techniques for "swagging" these things until after some trial-and-error methods. One morning I came bopping out of the dining hall with half-a-dozen Cheerios under my arm—and ran smack into the farm administrator. Shamefaced, I had to return them to the cereal rack. After doing so, he walked into the dining hall and bragged to the hacks on duty, "Ha, ha, I just caught Miller with an armload of cereal." Later, under the careful tutelage of a friend with years of experience at Macy's and Bloomingdale's, I learned to wear a shirt or jacket loosely and tuck the merchandise inside, around my waist. My friend, Marty, commented that I came to the penitentiary as green as a new kid on the block and would leave nickel slick.

After the 8:30 P.M. count at the farm camp, the kitchen was opened to let in the dairy crew that had done the seven o'clock milking. A few others might get in if they, for some reason, had worked late. These inmates were given a bag that normally contained two pathetic sandwiches of a single slice each of something that passed for lunch meat, and a couple of stale cookies: but they were also allowed two large dippers of milk. Depending on the whim of the night hack and his assistants, other inmates could get on the milk line. For one six-month period, the night officer permitted anyone to get milk. So, along with the crowd, I filled a glass jar that I had rescued from the dump, went back upstairs to my room, and ate my cereal. Good things never seem to last very long in prison and the milk ration came to an end. Many hacks are moved around in their jobs every six months precisely in order not to become too familiar with the inmates they work with. When this particular night hack was moved, one inmate made up a card saying that we were sorry to see him go but good luck, etc. I was among those who signed the card. The new night hack was much tighter.

Chapter 4 CORRESPONDENCE

In every prison, including military institutions, mail is censored by civilian employees of the institution. Presumably, mail is censored as a safeguard against escape, as well as the dissemination of gossip about other prisoners; neither justification suffices, for gossip can be disseminated and escape plans hatched during visiting hours. Another reason for censorship is to prevent the prisoner from pursuing his normal "employment" via mail during his incarceration. Of course, most Federal prisoners were involved in minor criminal activities which depended upon their actual presence at the scene. These were one-man operations. The few big-time operators can, no doubt, continue to exert authority despite mail censorship.

In all prisons, censorship is exercised not by the deletion of objectionable words (i.e., "foul" and "obscene" language) but rather by the total rejection of the letter in which this language occurs. This is sent back to the inmate or sender, together with an explanation for the rejection.

Mail call is held once a day, usually after evening chow, with Saturdays and Sundays not always, but usually, excluded. The domicile guard generally reads off the names of those inmates who have mail and hands the letters to them. By the time the inmate receives the letter it has been opened, because of its having been censored, and a staple has been used to partially reseal the envelope. In some prisons, mail is promptly processed and forwarded, but in others it is delayed for several days usually because of the small number of censors. Each domicile area has a mailbox and an inmate merely drops his unsealed letters off at his convenience; later, the box is emptied by the guard (who might, incidentally, read the mail) and its contents forwarded to the censor's office.

Every prison places some limitation upon the number of permissible correspondents an inmate may have; however, in many prisons non-approved parties may send mail to prisoners even though they are not permitted to receive mail from them. In most Federal prisons one is allowed twelve approved correspondents; in the military one is permitted five. In both prison systems married couples usually count as one correspondent. Most prisons do not permit prisoners to correspond with ex-Federal prisoners or, if the prisoner is married, with unmarried females.*

In military prisons the inmate is permitted privileged correspondence (i.e., uncensored, sealed letters) to and from lawyers of record, prospective (not yet retained) lawyers, and a clergyman from his community. In the Federal prison system these correspondents are not granted privileged status. In both Federal and military systems one is permitted privileged communications to various public officials (i.e., President, Vice-President, Attorney General, judges, Congressmen, Senators, Secretaries of the Army, Navy, Air Force, etc.). It should be mentioned, however, that even when privileged correspondence is permitted, it is not unheard of for prison officials to open, inspect, and read such correspondence. At the USDB one of the authors [H.L.] was placed in solitary confinement for a week because he had sent "contraband" to his lawyer. Prison officials had, prison regulations to the contrary, opened letters to and from his attorney. The "contraband" which so disturbed prison officials consisted of written

---

* As of July 1970, the ruling on correspondents was changed to include anyone except the wife or girlfriend of another prisoner or a prisoner in another institution.

material relating to the arbitrary censorship of the prison magazine. The material could hardly be considered contraband since a lawsuit challenging such censorship was actively being contemplated.

In all Federal and military prisons postage is paid for by the government on envelopes appropriately designated "Official Business."

Prior to the time that prison officials approve a prospective correspondent, the prison forwards this person a form to fill out; this form asks him to state his relationship to the prisoner. It is a good idea to forewarn prospective correspondents of this. Since it takes some time for these forms to be returned, the prisoner's choice of corresponddents is necessarily limited during the first few weeks of his incarceration. During this time, prison officials will usually permit correspondence only with immediate family members.

Your prison mailing list is your single most important link to the outside world and, in addition, it should provide you with the moral support to help you through those periods of "prison blues" which affect every prisoner at some time or other; it should, therefore, be selected with great care. Once you have prepared your list of correspondents and it has been approved by prison officials, it is true that you *may* alter the list at some later date; but some institutions impose limitations upon the number and frequency of such alterations. And in all institutions a delay of from two weeks to a month is required to process a new application.

We realize that the choice of people with whom you may wish to correspond represents a deeply personal matter; however, we think it important to provide the prospective inmate with a few general guidelines gleaned from our own experience. We have found that most political prisoners initially choose to correspond with immediate family members and close personal friends. After a few months of incarceration, however, the sheer dullness and uneventfulness of prison life make it increasingly difficult to maintain these correspondences which, all too often, degenerate into an exchange of pleasantries, homilies, and social inanities. Obviously, most political prisoners will wish to maintain some contact with their families and friends, but little is to be gained if the number of such correspondents prohibits the inclusion of others on the mailing list. In a strange way, prison *can* be a rewarding social and political experience, but to reap its full rewards one must receive a feedback from the outside world. Opinions will undoubtedly undergo profound revisions while one is imprisoned, but these changes will either be stifled or without direction unless the prisoner is able to communicate them to others who are interested in, and capable of critically analyzing and dissecting his newly conceived ideas. It has been our experience that old-time acquaintances and college friends do not serve this function. One will also find that it is advantageous to write to those people who can help with the legal aspects of one's case or prison experience, and who can provide access to the mass media. Again, old friends and relations often cannot do so.

For these reasons, as well as many others, it is probably advisable to include at least a few politically oriented people on the mailing list right from the start. Not only will they provide you with useful news of current happenings and concepts, but you will find that you will be providing them with the same service. It is frequently advisable to include a clergyman or two on the list. All clergymen have a political platform, at least as large and in many cases much larger than their own congregations. In addition, properly pre-selected clergymen can often arrange legal assistance and access to the mass media if this service should become necessary. Finally, prison censors are sometimes a little more reluctant to censor mail to clergymen, and thus the inmate's freedom of expression is less limited.

The prospective prisoner might think about his mailing list prior to entering prison and discuss with his prospective correspondents—family included—what assistance he expects or hopes to receive from them. We might note at this time that correspondents are permitted to send books; it would be advantageous to discuss with these people which books he wishes to receive.

Prisoners are permitted to receive greeting cards on all major and minor holidays. Generally speaking, prison censors will not reject a card if it contains a brief message; however, we are uncertain as to what might happen if this convenience were abused. At Christmas, most political prisoners receive an avalanche of cards, often totaling several hundred. These cards help to offset the Christmas depression which pervades all prisons. Once, though, a friend of the author [D.M.] sent a homemade card to him in prison. The friend, Ann Speltz, had made up a batch of cards for Father's Day with a quote from e. e. cummings on fatherhood to send to various imprisoned resisters. Apparently the censors at Lewisburg thought that e. e. cummings had sent [D.M.] a personal message. The card was returned to Ann Speltz's home addressed to E. E. Cummings and with a note that read, "We are sorry Mr. Cummings but you are not one of Mr. Miller's correspondents."

In general, the most frustrating and iniquitous censorship for prisoners is that which prohibits mention of adverse prison treatment and conditions. At times this prohibition reaches ludicrous proportions. In some prisons one is not even permitted to mention facts which relate to disciplinary action imposed on oneself. Prisons, as noted elsewhere, are the quintessence of "closed societies," and prison officials zealously guard prison secrets. In addition, in some prisons, radical political views are also sometimes censored. Two examples should highlight the problem. At Petersburg Federal Reformatory, one political prisoner was not permitted to advise his parents that he had been banished to disciplinary segregation; and at the USDB, letters which contained the words "political prisoner" were automatically censored. Letters which refer to specific prison abuses are almost certain to be rejected regardless of the truth or merit of the statements made. If one has access to an attorney, these restrictions—especially those which relate to the expression of divergent political views—can usually be circumvented. Sometimes, if a lawyer is not available, a clergyman can serve as a perhaps somewhat less effective, but nonetheless satisfactory substitute, in compelling prison authorities to pay passing attention to the Bill of Rights.

Some prisoners have used elaborate code systems in dealing with the censorship problem; for obvious reasons, we cannot detail these arrangements here. On the other hand, it is usually not too terribly difficult to smuggle letters out of prison. Again, we cannot comment on this; in any case, since the appropriate channels for smuggling differ from prison to prison, experience will prove to be the best guide in these matters. One word of caution· *do not abuse these methods for to do so invites disclosure.* Use them only when it is of the utmost importance to do so, and be discreet.

As a political prisoner one can expect his mail to be subject to a more intensive scrutiny than will be the case for nonpolitical prisoners. We do not know for certain but we have strong reason to believe that on occasion prison officials photocopy the letters of political prisoners. We have seen photocopied letters of nonpolitical prisoners which were stolen from official prison records. It therefore seems most likely that the mail of political prisoners is similarly dealt with. The inmate should therefore carefully avoid writing anything which may sometime in the future prove incriminating. If one finds that many letters are being returned, or if prison officials forbid correspondence with politically suspect friends, intervention by one's attorney frequently, but not always, resolves the snag. If one does not have access to an attorney, a letter to one's Congressman, Senator, or some other public official is sometimes of help, especially if one's complaint is, as is the case in political censorship, clearly directed against discriminatory and unreasonable practices.

One final word: almost all, if not all, prisons forbid prisoners to publish articles or books. Exceptions can be made by the warden, but they have never, to our knowledge, been made for political prisoners. Once again, this rule is easy enough to circumvent; however, the penalties, if one is caught, can be severe (maximum ten years). The inmate will have to use his own judgment on this score; correspondents, when properly selected, can be useful in this regard.

One political prisoner has written that in prison one "feels as if life were passing you by." This is surely true, but correspondents can do much to forestall this melancholy feeling. Choose them with care to make the best use of the mailing privilege.

(The following addendum is by David Miller.)

Near the end of my "bit" Catherine told me that she had
been saving all of my letters. She said she planned to
consolidate them and then mimeograph them on one side
of a sheet of paper: she was joking. Actually I wrote once
or twice a week but truthfully, the letters did not get
much longer than a page each. As I look back, I see that
my problem was twofold. Early in my prison experience I
was turned off writing long letters. I found it very repulsive that the deeply personal feelings between Catherine
and me (and between my other correspondents and me)
would be subject to the perusal of those who censor the
mail. I never became hardened to that. There is plenty
that happens in prison to write about—the problem is that
one is not permitted to write about what *actually* happens.
While at Allenwood I was called in to the caseworker's
office and asked to explain a letter I had written the day
before; it was to an approved correspondent, Marty Cor-
bin, the Managing Editor of the *Catholic Worker*. It contained negative opinions of the caseworker and the camp
superintendent, along with a criticism of my being refused
a visiting furlough in order to be present at the birth of my
second daughter: the interview was exasperating. The
camp superintendent said that I was not to write about
the personnel. I asked whether favorable opinions of him
and other personnel would have allowed the letter to get
out; he simply refused to answer. The caseworker was
disturbed about my saying things like, "If he [the case-
worker] doesn't want to listen to you, he turns off his
hearing aid." If I didn't understand where I was, the case-
worker was happy to remind me. He said, "I'm the case-
worker and you're the inmate, remember that." After that

encounter, I didn't write any more letters about prison happenings—at least not any that went through the regular channels.

Other inmates took different tacks. I don't know what personal matters they wrote about, but I do know that Howard Levy and Don Baty, for two, wrote long letters on political and social issues. Howard corresponded heavily with several political activists, including one or two at Health-Pac, in New York, where he was going to work after release. Don wrote long book reviews and critiques to his professor in a correspondence course given by Friends World College. I didn't correspond at length with anyone on political issues: I think this was a failing on my part. If I were forced to do another bit, I would write much more frequently than I did the first time. But I would be painfully aware—as would my correspondents—that our words were being duly noted.

Chapter 5   VISITING

Prison officials realize that visitors help to maintain prisoner morale and thus make their job of administration easier. But morale cannot be permitted to become too high because that would nullify the punishment component of imprisonment. Therefore, all prisons impose limitations on who may visit and the frequency of these visits. Exact rules and regulations concerning visiting vary from institution to institution. However, the generalities cited below are representative of the Federal prison system.

In most Federal prisons only immediate family members are permitted to visit. In a few prisons, family members may visit an unlimited number of days per month, but in most prisons visits may total only a few hours per month. At Lewisburg Federal Penitentiary the total time permitted visitors is three hours a month. This may be arranged so as to increase the total visits if not the total hours. Visitors are often permitted on both weekdays and weekends, although a few institutions restrict visiting to weekends. In general, weekday visits, when permitted, are best, because the visiting room is less crowded and officials are sometimes willing to overlook the time limitation.

At the USDB, any correspondent on the inmate's approved mailing list may visit; further, these visits are not limited to any specific number of hours per month. However, visiting at the USDB is limited to weekends only—unless the visitor has traveled a great distance and plans to stay for only a short time.

In Federal and military prisons all visits are conducted in a large, reasonably comfortable, though overcrowded room. Prior to entering the room, the prisoner is "shaken

45

down." The shakedown varies in thoroughness from prison to prison. In some prisons it involves only a quick frisk; in other prisons it consists of a strip-search as the prisoner is required to disrobe completely while a hack looks through his hair, in his mouth, under his genitals, between his buttocks, and at the bottom of his feet. The purpose of this search-and-psychologically-destroy operation is to insure the fact that no contraband is passed between prisoner and visitor. The procedure is, of course, repeated after the visit is completed. Despite the overkill involved in this operation, materials are still transferred.

After all of the inmates' orifices have been checked, he is permitted to enter the visiting room. There are no screens, windows, or bars between the inmate and the visitors. The prisoner is permitted to greet his visitors with a kiss or embrace but expression of affection beyond such greetings are prohibited. One USDB official, a Comstockian colonel, forbade the holding of hands under threat that if his sense of decency was again violated, he would ban all future visits.

In no Federal or military prison are visitors permitted to exchange gifts of any kind with prisoners, although, in Federal prisons, they are permitted to deposit money with the visiting-room clerk for the prisoner's commissary account.

Individuals who have had a previous Federal conviction are not permitted to visit prisoners.

In all prisons, lawyers of record, or prospective attorneys, are permitted to visit any day up to about 4:00 P.M. Sometimes a special room is provided for such visits but in some institutions these consultations are held in the regular visiting room.

At prison-farm camps affiliated with Federal penitentiaries visits are held within the prison walls. However, during the spring and summer months, weekend visits may be held at the farm camp itself. These visits are much more pleasant since they are conducted outside the dormitory building, on the lawn. A few political prisoners object to these visits on the grounds that the idyllic setting gives a misleading impression to visitors. This is probably true, but then the politeness and oversolicitousness of visiting-room guards *within* the walls of the prison has the same, though somewhat less intense, effect. Prison officials put on their best face for visitors, but short of refusing to receive all visits, an alternative for which few political prisoners have opted, the best that you can do about the situation is to explain the duplicity to your visitors.

Aside from visitors and correspondents, prisoners are virtually isolated from the outside world. On infrequent occasions, lawyers may be permitted to telephone prisoners, but phone calls to lawyers are not generally permitted. On several occasions when one of the authors [H.L.] was confronted with the possibility that he would be punished by prison officials with solitary confinement, and even threatened with a new court-martial, he was not permitted to telephone his attorney for advice.

Telephone calls from families are not permitted except in times of dire emergencies; i.e., serious illness or a death in the family. Telephone calls from inmates to their families are allowed, but infrequently. At times of death or an imminent death in the family, prisoners are usually permitted to visit home. Sometimes the prisoner is permitted a weekend visit unaccompanied by a guard, but most often he is under the supervision and surveillance of a guard.

Political prisoners are occasionally confronted with special problems concerning visitors. In general, clergymen are often permitted to visit prisoners; however, we know

of at least two instances in which this privilege was denied
to political prisoners. In one case, a political prisoner's
home-town minister traveled over a thousand miles to
visit, only to be turned away at the gates of the USDB.
Visitors whose unpopular political views are known to
prison officials may be denied visiting privileges. Likewise,
visitors whose physical appearance is unconventional may
be denied entrance to the prison. At the USDB, one of
the authors [H.L.] had the experience of having a few of
his visitors and correspondents—doctors and medical students—denied entrance to the visiting room because they
wore beards. A prison official told him that "such people
would offend the other visitors." Then he added, "And
besides, their political opinions are not good for your well-
being." Likewise, women wearing very short dresses or
skirts may be denied entrance. Although we are not yet
aware of it happening, we would assume that an obviously
braless woman's request to visit would be turned down.*

In some prisons, inmates may be permitted to exceed
their monthly quota of visitors, but often this principle
does not apply to political prisoners. Yet generalizations
are risky because at times a liberal attitude does prevail
for political prisoners.

The visiting situation does not provide the possibility
for meaningful communication: it is not meant to. What
can be said when one is limited to three hours a month,
sometimes a little more? Whether at the farm camp or in
the penitentiary, the visiting room is crowded with adults
and children. Husband and wife grow apart because they

---

* Our guess was correct. In August 1970 a guard at the USDB harrassed
and threatened to deny a braless woman her visiting privileges on the
grounds that she "did not meet the proper dress requirements." The
guard claimed that the woman would "torture" the prisoner by arousing
him sexually. It was only because this was to be her last visit before returning to the East Coast that the guard finally relented and allowed her
to visit the inmate.

are undergoing profound changes—especially if they are young—and they neither have the time nor the right atmosphere to communicate what is happening inside one another. The same is true for children, although their level of communication is very different. Two or three years of a child's life are enormously important in terms of personality development: there is no way in the world that a father in prison can relate to that growing child's emotional and physical needs. The only consolation that current visiting practices in Federal prisons bring is the opportunity for the inmate and his family to renew their faith in the existence of one another. Otherwise, visiting, as surely as imprisonment itself, functions to destroy family ties.

Something that we witnessed in the visiting room time and again illustrates the point. After being together for an hour or so, an inmate and his wife may spend the rest of the time staring off into space. They don't have anything more to say. In fact, they have everything to say—except that they can't bring themselves to say it. They don't want to appear to be complaining. Conversely, some inmates will talk continuously about anything under the sun in order to cover up their inability to hold a serious conversation.

The administration, at all times, strives to retain a convivial atmosphere in reference to the visiting procedures. But if a visitor tries to take a real interest in an inmate, look out! The administration doesn't want wives, mothers, or fathers to come to the penitentiary and demand to know what is happening to the prisoner. The officials don't want to hear this kind of talk, and if they can't frighten it off with a little tough talk of their own, they will solve the problem by shipping the inmate a thousand miles away. That usually ends the visits.

(The following addendum is by David Miller.)

An incident that occurred between the Protestant chaplain at Lewisburg and my wife, Catherine Miller, serves to put the administration's position straight. The background of the incident was at Allenwood. Almost from the time that I got there, Catherine and I had our run-ins with the visiting-room hacks. The first one happened when Catherine appeared on a visiting day and demanded to see me, even though she had used all her time for that month. She was eight months' pregnant, and had just seen off the wives of two other political prisoners at Allenwood who were on their way to visit their husbands after staying the night at her place. She arrived with our first daughter who was then a year and a half old. The visiting-room officer mishandled the affair and, among other things, threatened to call the FBI on my wife and our daughter. We were finally allowed to visit together for fifteen minutes; later, I was called in by the camp superintendent and asked to "control" my wife. After our second child was born, we had a couple of more run-ins. One was a brief argument with a different visiting-room officer about how long we could be together during a particular visit. (He had asked us to terminate our visit but we thought we should be allowed a longer time since the visiting room wasn't crowded.) Another scene occurred during the winter when I was helping Catherine and the children out the visiting-room door; the outside visiting area goes right up to the line of parked cars, and I was helping Catherine carry our infant daughter, our toddler, and some odds and ends to the car when a hack told me that I wasn't supposed to do that. Visits, he said, were to be terminated in the visiting room. I told him that the ground was icy and that I wasn't going to leave my wife to manage alone, over icy ground, with two small children and parcels. (The reader must bear in mind that Allenwood is a *minimum-security* honor camp.)

A few months later I was sent back to the penitentiary from Allenwood. When I got there I asked the Protestant chaplain to call Catherine for me, tell her where I was, and that I was all right. He did this, but added something of his own, as Catherine was later to tell me. He said, in essence, "Mrs. Miller, wouldn't it be possible for you to live somewhere else? With your mother or David's mother?" "But why?" said Catherine. "Well, they [obviously meaning the prison administration] think that David does harder time with you so close by and seeing him so often. They think he would be better off if you weren't around." "But the children and I came up here to be *able* to visit more often," said Catherine. "Well, they think that an inmate should forget about his family and the outside and do his time. When he gets out, he should pick up the pieces, wherever they are."

Before our second daughter was born, Catherine wrote to Washington requesting permission for me to be with her at the time of birth; she was living twenty miles away from Allenwood. She got a supporting letter from Dr. Robert Bradley, author of *Husband-Coached Natural Childbirth*. Dr. Bradley set forth his credentials, spoke of the benefits of natural childbirth, and said how important it was for the husband to be present at the birth. He concluded by saying that he thought the prison authorities should grant me a furlough. Washington wrote back saying that it had forwarded the request to the penitentiary, which reserved the right to make the decision. Soon after, a negative answer was received with the cryptic comment: "Furloughs are not being granted for that reason."

A few weeks later our daughter was born in a hospital not sixteen miles from Allenwood.

The law reads: "An extension of limits may be granted only to permit a visit to a dying relative, attendance at the funeral of a relative, the obtaining of medical services not otherwise available, the contacting of prospective employers, or for any other compelling reason consistent with the public interest. . . ." Obviously, being present at my daughter's birth—just sixteen miles away—was not a "compelling reason consistent with the public interest." But there were times when the authorities did decide that an extension of limits for a number of inmates did serve such a compelling reason. As when inmates were furloughed for Jaycee conventions and local softball games.

My wife lived near the penitentiary for nearly twenty months, renting a farmhouse in nearby Northumberland. She purposely rented a house larger than necessary for her and the children so that she might be able to provide hospitality to the visiting friends and relatives of prisoners. She did just that all the time she lived there. Although I made it known to some nonpolitical prisoner friends of mine that their relatives would also be welcome, only the relatives of political prisoners took advantage of the offer. Toward the end of my imprisonment, Catherine and I had thought out and come to believe in the need for a larger operation in the area; a bigger "house of hospitality" was needed if we hoped to relieve the needs of all prisoners and their families. The idea was twofold in nature.

First, there was the need itself. Many people find it difficult, if not impossible, to visit because they do not have the money for transportation and lodgings: it is especially hard on those who have to use public transportation and further complicated if there are children involved. For example, it takes five or six hours by bus to get from New

York to Lewisburg; when the bus arrives, visitors have to take a cab to the penitentiary. Add to this the fact that there is no longer a waiting room at the bus stop and the whole idea becomes discouraging. A permanent "house of hospitality" where visitors could find lodgings, a meal, a place to relax between buses, and a car service between the bus stop and the penitentiary would go a long way toward brightening up visits for many people.

Second, there was the political aspect involved in a larger "house of hospitality." A prison resistance movement cannot hope to succeed without *organized support on the outside* and ideally, this support should come from the communities adjacent to the prisons. In order to develop support, there has to be some line of communication between the people on the outside and the inmates. There is no more effective line than visitors; censorship of mail precludes any frank discussion of issues through that medium. The only way for local radical and liberal elements to know what is going on in the penitentiary is for visitors to report back to them after a visit. Thereafter, local supporters will gain the knowledge and information which they need in order to proceed. Hopefully, enough financial support for the house might be found in the general area. The techniques could be copied in the communities surrounding all the major prisons in the country—state, Federal, and military. We would then be in a position for concerted action.

Chapter 6   RECREATION

The greatest array of time-consumers and distractions in prison comes under this heading. We will take them one at a time and say a few words about each.

Television is big. Variety shows, sports colossals, movies, spy series, and police series are the biggest attractions. News programs have a hard-core audience. Political discussion programs are sparsely attended except when the theme deals with racial affairs—in which case a large audience, almost always entirely black, attends. The questionable pleasure of watching TV is diminished by the twenty to one hundred men sitting together. The usual schedule runs like this: on at 4:00 P.M., off at 11:00 P.M. on weekdays; on at noon and off at 1:00 A.M. on weekends. In some prisons, a prisoner program-selection committee chooses the shows to be seen; once chosen and scheduled the programs cannot be changed. In other prisons, such as the USDB, where this method is not used, altercations, sometimes of a serious nature, break out over TV selections.

Card-playing, dominoes, and Scrabble have their enthusiasts. There also develop regular groups for gin rummy, pinochle, bridge, bid a whist and the like. Bets are usually paid off with packs of cigarettes.

Most inmates are provided with a set of earphones with which they can listen to a choice of two, and sometimes three, local commercial radio stations. Every cell and most dormitory bunks are so wired for sound. Tapes and records are played for a few hours each evening over the prison monitor system. The schedule for this endeavor might run more or less as follows: Monday—Spanish music, Tuesday —hard rock, Wednesday—jazz, Thursday—bands and show tunes, Friday—soul, Saturday—country and western, Sunday—monitor's choice. On weekdays the radio is turned off at midnight or thereabouts. At least one station is on all day starting from about 6:00 A.M.

At the USDB, an occasional disc jockey, an inmate working for the prison radio station, was favorably predisposed to political prisoners and would insert as many politically oriented selections into his program as possible. These selections might include folk singers such as Phil Ochs and Pete Seeger, as·well as choices from some of the leading rock groups. Black disc jockeys would do likewise for black prisoners with rhythm and blues selections. Thus, songs like James Brown's "I'm Black and I'm Proud" were afforded very ample air time. Radio broadcasts, however, are taped and monitored by prison officials. Hence, the freedom offered the disc jockey is circumscribed. At the USDB, several black disc jockeys were fired because, according to prison officials, they played music which might have led to a riotous situation. Record playing on the one or two record-players available is a jealously guarded privilege. It falls into the hands of a record-room monitor or a phonograph monitor. There is supposedly a schedule so that everyone may have an equal chance, but that is not usually the case. Some monitors are better than others, but a particular clique wins out most of the time. Ill feelings have been known to arise because of this.

At many Federal prisons, inmates are permitted to receive records from friends and relatives outside. These must be sent direct from the recording company or retail store. They must be approved by prison authorities, although to the best of our knowledge a record has never been censored. In part, this may be due to the fact that political prisoners have made scant use of this privilege and have not attempted to import politically oriented recordings. Given the nature of the recording industry the pickings, in any event, would be slim.

There is a crowd of horn tooters, drum beaters, and guitar strummers, with always a couple of professionals around. They may even get together in a group. The majority of those fooling around with a musical instrument do just that.

An institution-sponsored movie is shown on Saturdays and Sundays. Westerns and spy films are the most popular. Ingmar Bergman, to say nothing of Jean-Luc Godard, does not appear, and certainly it will be some time before Andy Warhol makes his prison debut.

Concerning athletics, there is, of course, a great disparity between winter and summer. The farm camps have no inside gym facilities for winter use. Only the larger parent institutions provide some inside space and the inmates are obviously cramped. There *is* a gym for basketball, and a corner section is set aside for weight-lifting, ping-pong, and perhaps a handball court.

At the institutions which have an inside gym, there is an all-star basketball team made up of the best players from the intramural league. This team plays outside teams in the area, rounded up by the prison athletic director. There is one striking rule operative here. The Federal team must be integrated at all times, and there must be at least one white face on the court despite the fact that the majority of the best players is black.

Springtime brings the opening of the prison yard and a renewed interest in the outside facilities at the farm camps. Horseshoes, handball, track, volleyball, baseball, softball, basketball, weight-lifting, and in the fall, football, are all indulged in. As with basketball, outside teams are invited into the institution to play the all-star softball team. At the farm camps the all-star team is occasionally permitted to travel to play these outside teams. Indeed, the softball teams are the pride of the farm camps. Much time and considerable resources are devoted to the farm team to the detriment of the rest of the recreational programs, all done with the objective of sending the farm team on to the county and state tournaments—with all of the good publicity directed toward the prison. So concerned are prison officials with the success of its ball teams, that, as already mentioned, gifted players are actually transferred to the farm camps solely because their talents are needed there in order that the camp may field a superior and winning team.

Some political prisoners feel strongly that political prisoners should not lend their time and talents to the organized teams within the prison system. They object to the good image that the teams give to the institution, and further, feel that their time would be better spent in other endeavors. Certainly, non-organized sports such as handball, track, weight-lifting, etc., give the political prisoner ample opportunity to flex his muscles and maintain his physical condition. Then, too, the organized sports are clearly a method whereby prison officials deplete and exhaust all excess psychic energy which might, without these distractions, be turned against the prison system itself. This phenomenon extends beyond the actual playing field. There is a certain kind of pettiness in prison, unequaled outside, in reliving umpteen times over bad or questionable calls made by the umpires, and mistakes, errors, and misjudgments made by teammates. This pettiness can only be explained in terms of the distraction and emotional outlet it provides.

The other major recreation which all prisons provide is an arts and crafts center. Prisoners can make leather watch bands, pocketbooks, sandals, etc. They can paint by numbers or without, although the paint must be ordered and paid for by the inmates. A closer look at the prison art program may provide some insight into the function of all prison recreation activities.

The key to understanding prison arts and crafts programs is the realization that these activities are merely another diversionary tactic in the prison officials' arsenal. True creativity is discouraged, and as a consequence prison arts and crafts assume a bland and sometimes puerile pseudo-romantic look. In part, the prisoners' own conformist outlook prevents them from indulging in nonrepresentational painting and their artistic endeavors lean toward a literalness which amounts to little more than a copy of magazine photography. But if a given prisoner explores something different, his efforts are curtailed by prison authorities. At the USDB, certain subject matter was entirely taboo. Prisoner artists could neither depict the institution nor its staff in a critical manner, nor could they unfavorably represent the army, war, or aspects of American life in general. In fact, many canvases were criticized by officials because they were "too depressing." The sensual representation of women or sexual themes was also prohibited. What was true of the USDB also seems to be true, in greater or lesser degree, of all Federal prisons.

Essentially then, what these interdictions amount to is that the prisoner artist is not permitted to express anything which might be of importance to him. He cannot aesthetically examine his predicament, and any talent he might possess is effectually suppressed. Prison policy thus prevents the inmate from freeing himself through the medium of artistic expression: the prisoner's mind as well as his body must be kept behind bars.

But it is doubtful that prison officials possess the nimbleness or subtlety of mind to be conscious of this double imprisonment. Rather, prison officials are simply aesthetic philistines and are intuitively frightened by anything which smacks of artistic originality or sincerity. From time to time a prison official will "commission" a work from a prisoner, most often a family portrait. Prisoners are happy to oblige because they are usually paid twenty-five to fifty dollars for the painting. These "commissioned" works are usually copied from photographs, and never have any artistic merit. They do, however, satisfy the pedestrian tastes of prison officials.

Some Federal prisons hold an annual art show. Aside from the money which the inmate may derive from the sale of his paintings and handiworks, these exhibitions make for a sad display. One prominent art critic decided from a perusal of the exhibition's brochure that she had best not waste her time attending the display at Leavenworth Federal Penitentiary. Indeed, only those critics who are consummate masochists would expose themselves to such punishment, for prison art shows are very depressing affairs.

It would only be fair, though, to point out that there are men and women in prison who are gifted artists. But these select few, many of whom "blossomed" during their incarceration, are exceptions who developed against great odds. And from conversations with fellow inmates, the consensus is that the best in-born prison artists are in state penitentiaries.

(The following addendum is by David Miller.)

The political prisoners at Allenwood did not, as a group, distinguish themselves on the athletic field. There were a few who stood out: Dick Cool, Roger Johnson, and I. A few tried but lacked the talent. The strongest feeling pervading a very large percentage of the political prisoners was an eschewing of a hard, competitive athletic spirit—a most un-American trait. Volleyball was a favorite sport among these latter, but if the game became "too" competitive, they would leave. It was really quite rare to find a political prisoner with both the talent and the willingness to be a member of a prison team that faced nonprison teams. The question of athletics as easygoing enjoyment or keen competition, and that of whether or not to represent a penal institution involve substantial personal and political analysis: I don't want to examine those questions here. I must say that when I play I play hard and to win, and that I did represent the institution on its basketball and softball teams: it was a dubious honor, but I enjoyed it.

The Jehovah's Witnesses were different, being highly competitive, with a number of good athletes among them. Most of them also followed professional sports very closely. Once, at a basketball tournament around Thanksgiving, I managed to put together a team of political prisoners and a renegade JW: we "sold a lot of tickets" (made challenges) but lost to a JW team despite the strong efforts of political prisoners Steve Reid and Rod Alexander. We probably could have won had not Dick Cool chosen to play for a team organized by the Muslims. I remember the day well: we beat a weaker JW team in the morning by the absurd score of 12 to 6. I'd never been in a game like that before; the temperature was in the forties and we were playing on an outdoor court since there are no indoor facilities at Allenwood—save for a ping-pong table. The wind played havoc with the cheap basketball we had. In the afternoon the temperature went up, we got a better ball, and the scores were more respectable.

I played softball almost daily during the summer I was

at Lewisburg. I had a good glove but weak arm in center field and needed much practice at the plate. However, I did hit the first home run of the year—although it was to be my last. The high point of the season was beating Allenwood, since it was the first time that Lewisburg had ever done so. We played at home and our pitcher gave a superb performance. I made six or seven catches that should have been routine except that I had to tiptoe through the sea of mud that covered half of center field. (My counterpart did not fare as well. Roger Johnson was playing center field for Allenwood, and took a healthy spill in the mud early in the game.) The return game at Allenwood was our disaster: hardly any of us had our minds on it. Traveling to Allenwood was an opportunity to visit with friends that we hadn't seen for months; when we were at bat I spent my time on the sidelines talking with some of the political prisoners. There was a great deal to talk about since I had not seen any of them since my transfer. In the intervening period there had been the rape of a young Selective-Service violator. We didn't get much said, but we tried.

Another "first" at Lewisburg was that the camp was allowed to place a basketball team in the intramural league inside the wall. When we came inside and started "smokin'" they were sorry: in regular season play we tied for the championship.

Penitentiary basketball is not, to say the least, well organized. It's a run-and-shoot game with wild passes and many turnovers. One of its distinguishing features is the tight control the referees exercise over it. Anything that vaguely resembles a foul is called; any show of emotion or disgust, or a swear word, is a technical foul; two technicals and you are out of the game. The reason for this is the highly combustible setting; it would be simple for a fight between two players to spread to both teams and then to the whole gym. All the time I played I never saw a full-fledged fight between players, although there were many that were close. I never saw or even heard of anyone hitting a referee either during or after a game; it certainly wasn't that they didn't provide cause. It was the triumph of the better judgment of the players who knew that such an act would cause them to be locked in segregation, at the very least, or charged with inciting to riot in a congregated area, at the very most. I personally was ejected from games on several occasions.

We played under college rules, and between the intramural league and all-star games once a week, I must have played thirty-five games that season: that's a lot of basketball. I had great personal duels with a white ballplayer friend. We were unofficially vying to be best "whitey" in the joint. He lost, but it might have been different had I not had the youthful advantage.

Most inmates stop playing organized sports a month or two before they're released; they don't want to go home with a broken ankle or the like. I played up until the day I left because the guys at the farm camp wanted to win the league and my 22 points a game couldn't be dispensed with. If the referees and the recreation director didn't take it from us, we wanted to win. Unfortunately, the season ended in a tie on a Tuesday: I was to leave Friday morning. The recreation director scheduled a three-game playoff starting the day after my release. Some of the guys joked about trying to play the first game at eight o'clock Friday morning, before I left. Inside the wall, a brother panned me by saying he had heard that I'd asked to stay a few more days.

The afternoon before I left I passed by the industries building on my way to R&D (Receiving & Discharge), and ran into several of the ballplayers I knew. One of them, Levi (a brother from Washington, D.C., and the best basketball player in the joint), shook my hand and said, "Good luck, man, I know you're going out there and tell them what it's like here." But what could I do for Levi, who is doing a twenty-year bit? What could I do for the other ballplayers, and the other inmates I knew? Nothing, except continue the struggle. I said, "Yeah, man, I'm going to do that."

Chapter 7   SERVICE ORGANIZATIONS

The Jaycees are the largest of the service groups within the prison. The prison chapters are entirely separate and fullfledged members of the nationwide Junior Chamber of Commerce, and are organized to promote "community spirit." They, as with other prison service groups, are emasculated beyond redemption. The old-timers informed us that the chapter at Lewisburg Penitentiary was brought into the institution by an FBI agent who also happened to be a member of the local Jaycee chapter in the Lewisburg area. This story may be apocryphal but it does say something about the organization's mode of operations.

The organization's propaganda reads that the Jaycees do this, the Jaycees do that, they become active, they take an interest in others. But what do the Jaycees actually accomplish?

They bring in an occasional movie.

They take polaroid color snapshots of prisoners and their loved ones (for a dollar fifty) in the visiting room.

They take trips to clean up or repair nearby charitable institutions, and they take trips to nearby Jaycee conventions. These trips are few and not all Jaycee members are permitted to go. Usually two or three of the most trustworthy inmates, in the administration's judgment, are chosen for any particular trip. The prison administration must be absolutely sure that these inmates will not embarrass them in any way; the inmates who go live up to this expectation.

At Lewisburg there was recently a horrendous newspaper article posted on the Jaycee bulletin board. Two inmates, a bank robber and a dope pusher, were photographed while attending a Jaycee convention some distance away from the institution. They were reported as saying that prison was tough but that the Jaycees gave new hope and Warden Parker was as helpful as he could be. Warden Parker, they said, would give prisoners any possible break. This is sheer propaganda. As we have said, Jaycee convention-bound delegates are carefully screened.

The photographs which the Jaycees take in the visiting room yield several hundred dollars of profit each year. Some of this profit is used to supply the free coffee which is served visitors, and some pays for the Jaycees' movies. As might be expected, prison officials are the Jaycees' biggest boosters, and officials have let it be known that joining the Jaycees will not hurt a prisoner's chances of receiving a parole. However, the chances of a political prisoner receiving an early parole by joining the Jaycees are nonexistent.

The Jaycees sometimes operate the prison "radio" station. The latter is, in reality, a programed, two-hour tape that is played over the prison monitor system. The station often broadcasts public-service announcements for the Holy Name Society and Red Cross. Censorship, however, is strict: when a prisoner at Lewisburg asked the Jaycees to run an announcement concerning an ACLU investigation of prisoner treatment and rights the radio station declined the offer. To paraphrase W. C. Fields, "that's carrying public service a bit too far." (Or, in this case, too near.)

Most prisons publish a newspaper or a magazine. The contents of these publications almost invariably include "spiritual uplift" articles on Alcoholics and Narcotics Anonymous, religious guidance, announcements of forthcoming movies or radio shows, news of institutional athletic events and perhaps a few of general interest. The style and tone is unique to prison. "C'mon guys, return the sugar containers or we might have to get it on the line. Think of the other fella." As one might expect, prisoners, in private conversations and correspondence, do not talk or write in that style. Prison newspapermen are merely offering prison officials that which they have come to expect and implicitly demand: it's as if prison officials demand that prisoners live up to a stereotypical image of themselves as depicted in a poor parody of a Grade B movie script.

In those institutions which do publish a monthly magazine, prison officials are inordinately proud of the quality of these publications. Their joy is well-founded, since these magazines serve as yet another example of the penal system's public-relations program. In many institutions, the magazine is distributed to public officials and other opinion-molders as well as to the prisoners, and the latter are encouraged to send a copy to "the folks back home."

From a technical point of view some of these publications are of high quality. While they rarely reach the technical excellence of commercial magazines, they do reflect credit upon the prison magazine staff and printers. In general, the mood conveyed by the magazines' contents is one of high optimism and good cheer. It need hardly be stressed that the mood does not at all reflect the overall emotional climate which pervades these institutions, and the prison publications' misleading optimism is predicated upon the presence of the ever-watchful censor's eye.

As might well be imagined, the censor's hand rests heavily upon the editorial staff. Every article must be approved by the prison hierarchy prior to publication. Articles dealing with sex are, of course, taboo; articles which take a critical attitude toward the government or the institution itself will never see print. However, these remarks do not pertain to all *state* penal institutions, where considerably greater candor of expression is sometimes tolerated.

At the USDB, political prisoners were often tempted to work for the magazine. At that institution the most notorious political prisoners are forbidden such employment, but one occasionally slipped by and did his best to breathe some life into that institution's insipid monthly, *Stray Shots.* Efforts in this direction were uniformly unsuccessful and before long the attempt was abandoned. Nonetheless, at the USDB, magazine staffers who shared the perspectives of political prisoners were able, on occasion, to slip a political message past the censors. Thus, a photograph of contented soldiers accompanied an article dealing with basic training. In the center of the photo was Che Guevara: it was a photograph of Cuban revolutionists. On another occasion, a Fourth of July cover consisted of a highly stylized group of American revolutionary soldiers, muskets in hand, depicted against an abstract image of the American flag. To the right of the musketeers was a huge, mushroom-shaped cloud of smoke. In another issue of *Stray Shots,* the inside back cover contained the usual monthly calendar, together with a photograph of a military sword with a feather placed on each side of it. The design was unmistakably that of the traditional peace emblem.

The problem, however, with such examples of "underground journalism" is that it is of significance to only a handful of politically oriented prisoners. And while there is a certain satisfaction in outwitting the censors, in political terms the effort amounts only to game playing.

Prisoners who have tried to change things have had basically unsatisfactory results. At the USDB, one of the authors [H.L.], along with several black prisoners, attempted to compel prison officials to publish an issue of *Stray Shots* devoted exclusively to Afro-America. The effort failed and eventually resulted in his being banished to disciplinary segregation for a week. More successful was his effort, while working in the print shop, at sabotaging all photographs, earmarked for *Stray Shots*, having to do with the glorification of the military. Such photos uniformly were blurred, murky, and at times, indecipherable.

Chapter 8

The men and women who are provided by prison authorities to look after the spiritual welfare of the inmates do not challenge the concept of imprisonment, nor do they even attempt to propose innovations which might serve to dull some of its sharp edges. Instead, they actively support the present system or are silent.

The liturgy of worship and the religious counseling offered by the prison chaplains are under careful scrutiny by prison officials. Though their styles may sometimes differ, all of the chaplains cooperate. The real spiritual needs of inmates for a community of worship cannot be met so long as this spirit of acquiescence persists. There is no basis for equality between the minister and his congregation; there is no opportunity for frank discussion at the liturgy, nor is there reason to be frank in personal counseling sessions. For all these reasons, and many more, the spiritual community is doomed from the start.

The homilies given out by the prison chaplains differ only in greater or lesser shrillness; they are all circumstantial. If chaplains spoke to the needs of their congregations and acted in favor of them, they would not be tolerated by prison officials. Those things which are within the power of the chaplains to do for the members of their flock jeopardize neither themselves nor the institution. These might include getting out an uncensored letter, making recommendations for parole hearings, attending the funeral of a family member, and rarely, making a phone call. A desperate man is thankful for such favors, but favors only distract from more important considerations.

Considering the size of prison populations, church services are sparsely attended. It is a tribute to the hardheaded reality of the majority of inmates that this is the case: there is nothing in it for them.

Common practice has both a permanent Catholic and Protestant chaplain at every major institution. A paid rabbi in the area of the institution makes a weekly appearance for the benefit of the Jewish inmates. The Protestant chaplain is placed in charge of the remaining non-Catholic religious sects, although he is not the officiating minister. These sects include the Muslims and the Jehovah's Witnesses.

Muslims are permitted to conduct services in most Federal prisons. At the time of this writing, their right to do so has not been recognized by military-prison officials. Even in Federal prisons, the Muslims are harassed more than the other religious groups If a man wishes to convert to the Muslim religion, he must go through the Protestant chaplain; the latter has the power to approve or deny the inmate's request. Sometimes he chooses to deny and Muslim meetings are closed to that man.

The Jehovah's Witnesses hold their semi-weekly meetings and Bible-study groups with pretty much the full cooperation of the prison administration, for there is little reason for the administration to worry. Jehovah's Witnesses are the most cooperative prisoners imaginable. This behavior is a group decision and, supposedly, is because of religious convictions and principles.

At first glance, prison Protestant religious services are not all that much different from any other. The Sunday worship includes organ, choir, and printed program. From time to time at Lewisburg Federal Penitentiary, Catholic nuns were given a stipend to come in on Sunday. What is lacking is the feeling that the prisoners or the chaplains attend out of a sense of religious devotion, although undoubtedly there are a few exceptions. Most prisoners who attend church do so because they feel that their attendance may later help them get paroled. Most chaplains attend because they are paid to do so.

Prison officials are observant of religious holidays. On Christmas, for example, special meals are prepared. At the USDB, turkey with all the trimmings was the menu for Christmas as well as for national holidays such as Independence Day and Thanksgiving. During the holiday season Christmas trees and decorations are displayed, and the chaplain section may even pipe Christmas music over the public address system. Again, at the USDB, a huge, lighted cross was erected atop the main institution. Most of the political prisoners thought that, given the location, such conspicuous religionism was grotesque.

Jewish prisoners are provided with special Passover services and a Seder. On the other hand, food prepared in accordance with dietary laws are provided for neither Jewish nor Muslim prisoners.

Holiday celebrations in prisons fulfill an important role, aside from their ostensible relationship to the specific occasion. During the Christmas season a definite and noticeable air of heaviness and depression settles down upon the prison population. The season conjures up remembrances of family, loved ones, and happier days, long suppressed from memory; as a result, tensions begin to build and prison officials are alerted to the possibility of riots. During the 1968–69 Christmas season, guards at the USDB were on twenty-four-hour-a-day riot alert. In this context, the vain attempt at re-creating the festive atmosphere which normally might prevail on these occasions, can be seen as being directed toward soothing depression-prone and tension-ridden men. But prisons are dreary and psychologically cold. The warmth and joyous atmosphere which is so characteristic of Christmas at home cannot be re-created by hanging tinsel and colored lights on barred windows and doors. Nor does the slick and convivial chicanery of the new breed of prison chaplains bridge the distance between prison and home. The tough, "one-of-the-guys" prison chaplain of Hollywood fame is no longer in vogue; he has been replaced by the smooth, soft-spoken, folksy, benign clerical. The syrupy approach is used almost exclusively with political prisoners. This is important because it is symptomatic of still-evolving changes in the approach of prison officials to all prisoners, but especially to political prisoners. The Protestant chaplain at Lewisburg and Allenwood was a gifted exponent of the soft-sell religious experience.

He was in charge of the group-therapy gatherings at Allenwood Farm Camp, which a good portion of the political prisoners there attended. The chaplain was immediately identified as a "good guy." He offered sympathy—not much—but enough to be thought of as a friend, and perhaps even as a kind of ally. He brought in an occasional movie and musical group, and, once in a great while, a guest lecturer. Once in a while he got through a politically objectionable publication. He said that he was not an activist but, no matter, he would listen.

What, in fact, he did, was to act as a conciliatory agent between the administration and the political prisoner, as well as between the administration and the other prisoners; his presence and concern reduced antagonisms and pressures. Upon reflection, we believe he was entirely conscious of this role, although we did not challenge him at the time. In this guise, the chaplain is dangerous to the performance and development of the political prisoner, and the danger lies in not recognizing his true position and role. The question is not whether to relate to him or not, rather, it is to be *certain* to relate to him in terms of his actual function.

A case in point: the chaplain arrived in the segregation cell occupied by two political prisoners the morning after they were dragged in from Allenwood for refusing to do meaningless "make work"; a friendly face after a trying twenty-four hours. The first prisoner, one of the authors [D.M.], told him that he would go back to Allenwood and do the assigned work. An hour later, the chaplain had conveyed the message, and the two prisoners were brought before the associate warden. The warden made some thinly veiled threats concerning transfer to the boondocks (that is, to another prison in the middle of Nowhere, U.S.A.), and prosecution for inciting to riot. Finally, it was decided to send the first back to Allenwood. The second political prisoner reacted differently. He said he would work when and where it suited him: he might work, he might not. The chaplain broke in to conciliate. Would the second prisoner agree to be responsible for certain work if the hours were flexible? It was at this point in the discussion that the chaplain made his only serious blunder of identification. He said, "You see, what we are trying to work out with you . . ." *Voilà!* The "we" was not lost on the prisoner. That is the reality, and do not forget it.

An incident at the USDB will serve to strengthen the point. At a newly organized Unitarian service which utilized ministers from outside the institution, and filled prison officials with fear, there came, in the middle of the service, a loud, booming voice from the left side of the room. It was obvious that someone had pressed the wrong button—to be more exact the replay button—of a tape recorder. After the sermon, a prisoner arose and said that everyone knew that there was a tape recorder on that side of the chapel. Whereupon the Protestant chaplain, a major, got out of his seat, and with wires dangling, as it were, from beneath his jacket, beat a hasty retreat.

On the occasion of another Unitarian-Universalist Church service at the USDB, one of the authors [H.L.] demanded of the institution's chief chaplain, a colonel, that he approve the right of every inmate to attend Unitarian services, as well as the right of Unitarian inmates to distribute religious literature outside the chaplain's office—as was the custom for other religious groups within the prison. The chaplain replied that he could not make that decision but would "have to take it up" with the commandant (i.e., warden) of the prison.

On still another occasion, a tape recorder was discovered hidden behind, as the Unitarian minister was later to phrase it, "the veil of God." It had been placed there by a chaplain's assistant on orders from the chief chaplain.

A final example should clinch the argument. On April 23, 1969, an article appeared in the *National Catholic Reporter* which was entitled, "Discipline by Rape at U.S. Prison." The article alleged that authorities at Lewisburg Federal Prison were threatening political prisoners with "discipline by rape" should they step out of line (*see* "Homosexuality"). On May 9, 1969, "A Proclamation" together with a petition form was circulated among the officers of the prison's Holy Name Society and the Buffalo Valley Jaycees (*see* "Service Organizations"). The proclamation was addressed to Myrl Alexander, then director of the Federal Bureau of Prisons, and actively supported by the Catholic chaplain at Lewisburg Penitentiary. After exonerating prison officials from any responsibility for prison homosexuality, and denying the charge that officials were attempting to intimidate political prisoners by threat of rape, the proclamation concluded as follows: "In summation, therefore, we are convinced that the [*National Catholic Reporter*] article is part of a deliberately contrived smear campaign, designed to embarrass the United States and the Federal Prison System, and to elicit public sympathy toward the cause and plight of the conscientious objectors." With only a single exception, the officers of the above-named societies refused to sign the shamefully apologetic document, but the role of the Catholic chaplain, as exemplified by this episode, should be crystal clear. He was on their side, not ours.

The believer must look for spiritual nourishment elsewhere than the officially sanctioned service. The spiritual minister of a prison community must be one of its own, freely chosen from and by the community; he and the community must dynamically affirm their dignity in the face of the indignity offered them.

One word of caution! Those prisoners, who in good conscience attend the services offered by the prison, are to be respected. The prison, *not* prisoners, should be opposed.

Chapter 9   EDUCATION

FORMAL

Education programs, together with employment and psychotherapy, make up the three sides of the pyramid which is the hallmark of the new "rehabilitative" approach to imprisonment.

Since, for the most part, members of affluent families do not often find themselves in prison and further, since the level of educational attainment varies directly with family, social, and economic status, it should shock no one to learn that many prisoners are educationally underdeveloped. Prison education programs reflect these deficiencies—which affect a goodly minority, if not a majority, of the prison population. To be sure, even were we to exclude political prisoners, a few college-educated inmates can be found in every prison; but these inmates comprise an insignificant minority of the total population.

The cornerstone, therefore, of the prison educational program is an Adult Basic Education (ABE) curriculum. This course of daily instruction culminates with an examination which amounts to a composite of questions dealing with basic high-school course work. Upon the passing of this exam, the inmate is awarded a General Equivalency Degree (GED). This diploma is recognized by most of the states of the Union. On the other hand, it is not invariably recognized by future employers or by colleges and universities. Some prisoners are coerced into taking the ABE course, allegedly for their own good, but actually because prison officials feel that the greater the number of GED's attained, the better prison records are made to appear in terms of the fulfillment of the prison's rehabilitative mission. In passing, we should also mention that most prisons offer vocational-training programs in such trades as carpet laying, masonry, and welding. Most political prisoners do not participate in vocational training programs both because they are not encouraged to do so by the authorities and also because they themselves tend to be disinterested.

The following description of full-time prison educators does not necessarily pertain to recent college graduates who sometimes seek in-prison teaching positions as a short-run means of earning a few dollars before they embark upon their life's career. However, if such an instructor should, for idealistic reasons, seek to make prison teaching his career, the chances are that unless he were able to adjust his thinking and acting to the pre-set mold of his prison education-department superiors, he could not last more than six months before being fired.

The mentality of prison educator careerists can best be described as <u>antediluvian.</u> In general, their competence would never earn them tenure at a first-rate suburban public school. Furthermore, their political and social instincts are of a piece with the John Birch Society's *Blue Book*.

At the USDB, it was the broad consensus of that institution's educators that political prisoners ought be "lined up against the wall and shot." One instructor vowed to "kill with his bare hands" one of the authors of this book [H.L.] if he dared set foot in the Education Department. He did and came out of it unscathed. It was standard policy at the USDB to prohibit political prisoners from teaching and one was told that the reason he would not be permitted to teach was because he had committed a crime of "moral turpitude." His "crime" was to have refused an order to fight in Vietnam. Meanwhile, the same Education

Department employed two other prisoners, one of whom was convicted of sodomizing a troop of Boy Scouts and the other of having raped his pre-adolescent daughter.

That professional educators whose moral judgments are so perverted fail to impress or teach many prisoners is not surprising. They fare even worse with black prisoners for the reason that virtually all prison pedagogues are uninhibited racists. We might expect inmate instructors, who are used in all prisons to supplement the regular staff, to do better; but often this is not the case. In all too many instances, those prisoners who possess the academic credentials that enable them to land a teaching job demonstrate airs of superiority over their fellow prisoners. They are impatient, abrupt, and condescending to those prisoners who fail to progress at the speed expected of them. These failings are less marked when—the USDB excepted —political prisoners are permitted to teach. But even political prisoners are sometimes haughty and, more significantly, cannot empathize with most prisoners, again especially blacks, except on an abstract and intellectual level. None of this counts for very much since most prison curricula are devised only to help the prisoner obtain his GED. For this purpose, courses are GED-test oriented; academic learning is conveniently bypassed since it serves no utilitarian purpose. After all is said and done, a prisoner can obtain his GED for the price of two cartons of cigarettes paid to the right person in the Education Department.

Some prisons offer regular college courses. These are generally freshman- and sophomore-oriented and again are not rewarding for those political prisoners who have already completed several years of college. At the USDB, a unique program was available, which, if pursued long enough, could yield a degree from a local institution, High-

land Junior College. Political prisoners who have not been
to college could conceivably benefit from this type of program; however, they should be forewarned that many colleges and universities may not accept all of the credits obtained from such courses.

Of greater interest to political prisoners may be the
occasional college seminars and inmate-initiated courses
which can be found at most institutions. The seminars are
usually taught by professors from nearby colleges and the
subjects offered depend wholly upon the interests of the
volunteering professors. As a result, these programs are of
a catch-as-catch-can nature and generalizations regarding
them cannot be offered.

Prisoner-initiated courses, like the seminar programs,
are not offered for college credit, but at times, can be of
interest to political prisoners. At the USDB a prisoner with
a degree in psychology offered a course in clinical psychology. And at the same institution a new black studies course
was in the planning stage at the time of this writing.* At
Lewisburg Penitentiary a former Washington, D.C., slum-
lord offered a course on real estate. Prison censorship and
control (at the USDB the classrooms were bugged) in-
sures the fact that none of these courses will even vaguely
resemble a free university; from time to time, however,
stimulating ideas may seep through.

Almost all Federal and military prisons offer university
correspondence courses. Most often, the prison will have
a pre-established list of schools from which inmates may
choose course work. School catalogues are available in the
Education Department and can be reviewed upon request.
In most institutions prisoners are expected to pay their
own tuition; however, the military prisons do offer special

---

* The course was started and has since been discontinued. Prison officials
feared it might lead to a "race riot."

rates which effect considerable savings. Were a political prisoner interested in a subject not available through those colleges with which the institution had already an established working relationship, he might arrange, through the prison Education Department, a correspondence course with another school. One political prisoner at Lewisburg Farm Camp has received permission to take a course entitled "War and Peace—What Are the Prospects?" from Friends World College.

Most, if not all, Federal and military prisons have libraries that are most often under the control of the Education Department. These libraries are small and leave much to be desired for the serious student. Aside from fairly adequate sections containing compendiums on law, reference material is relegated mainly to encyclopedias and world almanacs. Mass-circulation magazines and newspapers are often available and go about as far to the left politically as the *Saturday Review, Harpers,* and *The Atlantic Monthly.* Fiction and nonfiction books will be found on the shelves, although recent titles may be hard to come by. Prison librarians seem to order books in a helter-skelter style and in all institutions financial support for libraries is inadequate.

An incident which occurred at the USDB may help to underscore the reasons why socially and politically relevant books are markedly scarce in prison libraries. Two prisoners [one of them H.L.] attempted to contribute books, free of charge, to the USDB library. A black prisoner offered a dozen books dealing with Afro-American history and Levy offered books mostly about the urban crisis (among them *110 Livingston Street,* which dealt with the New York City school bureaucracy). The library committee rejected all of the books on the grounds that such books "would contribute to a race riot at the institution." To the best of our knowledge, this was the only time the library committee took any action other than to rubber-stamp selections made by the librarian. In this instance, the librarian, a warm and genuine human being, had pre-approved the books in question, only to have his judgment overruled.

In general, prison officials and librarians prefer books which provide escapist themes (in the psychological, not physical sense). The only exception seems to be that overtly sexual themes are avoided, and it is said that literature dealing with violence is frowned upon; this latter stricture is dubious. Mysteries and books on crime line the shelves of prison libraries, and books containing graphically etched descriptions of violent crimes (such as *In Cold Blood*) are readily available.

It may be premature to generalize upon possible new developments concerning prison library facilities but for what it is worth, we will describe Lewisburg Penitentiary's new policy regarding its library. One year ago that prison's library contained 17,000 volumes. Today it contains several hundred. Thousands of books were removed from the library to make room for a "learning center." Although some of the books were sent to local prison-farm camps, nobody is certain about what exactly happened to most of them. One rumor is that the books were burned. If true, we have a unique case in which teaching machines and language tapes—which make up the "learning center"—have been substituted for books. Aside from the "learning center," which at the present consists of a single teaching machine, other explanations have been offered to explain the demise of the library. For a time, it was rumored that prison officials intended to exchange the hard-cover books with paperbacks which, so the line went, would be made more accessible to prisoners in domicile areas, and which would be easier and less expensive to keep up to date. Indeed, an initial attempt was made to do just this but the effort soon petered out; now, almost no decent reading matter is available to the average prisoner. One last explanation says that the library had been the scene of so many fights between inmates that removing the books would, by removing the prisoners' interest in the library, bring a halt to the hostilities. It would seem that if the "learning center" ever services more than the handful of prisoners who now use it, the problem will erupt again.

In some prisons the library may be supplemented by the personal library of the prison chaplain. Most prison chaplains are more than happy to allow prisoners to borrow their books and on occasion one may find several excellent titles.

In general, then, prison-education programs offer a few tidbits for a few prisoners. Some inmates undoubtedly profit from earning their GED, others learn potentially valuable work skills in vocational training programs, and a few may subsequently make use of college credits that they were able to pick up during their confinement.

But nobody should assume that these programs, in their totality, even begin to chip away at the encrusted layers of social abuse and neglect which lead to criminal pursuits in the first place. We have not encountered a single example of a prison-education program which might foster an understanding and, hopefully, an amelioration of prisoners' maladaptive life styles; or perhaps to state the case more accurately, to the maladaptive society against which they are compelled to struggle.

For political prisoners the options are even leaner. Formal prison-education programs are clearly not geared to political prisoners, and if the latter profit at all from them, they do so accidentally and not because the prison authorities structured any part of the program with their interests in mind.

SELF-EDUCATION

In theory, long prison hours, an excess of "free" time, and an absence of responsibilities, should allow political prisoners ample time to read and study. In practice, while prison does exclude many of the distractions which pervade social life outside of prison, new distractions are substituted. Many political prisoners have found them to interfere with serious study. Silence in prison is as rare as diamonds, and some men have found the noise to be an insuperable barrier to study. Without a doubt, the cacophony which results from high-volume TV sets, radio jacks, phonographs, card games, conversations, PA systems, and so on can be very disconcerting. Few prisons provide special rooms for reading and writing. On the other hand, some prisoners are ultimately able to "blank out" the dissonance and treat it as background noise much the same way that city residents learn to ignore street noise. At Lewisburg Prison Farm Camp, two prisoners requested that a small, quiet room be set aside for serious reading and study. As was true of the great majority of such requests, it was turned down without explanation.

A more fundamental problem is that some political prisoners do their "bit" (i.e., prison sentence) operating on what might be vaguely termed a state of low-level "situational depression." Laboring under this mental set precludes the likelihood of serious study, and in its stead we find that many political prisoners, like the general inmate population, squander away nearly all of their time with meaningless distractions such as TV, movies, athletic events, etc. The experiences, however, of a minority of political prisoners attest to the fact that these adverse circumstances can be overcome. Some political prisoners have profitably used their prison time for the purpose of political self-education, and it is to this subject to which we will now turn our attention.

Political self-education and prison resistance (*see* "Resistance") form the cornerstone of an effective and sanity-preserving approach to imprisonment. Self-education in prison can be thought of as a multilevel, multidimensional affair. On one level, it consists of solitary reading and writing. On a second level, the books read and the letters written can be discussed with other political prisoners. And on a third level, political studies can become a collective activity involving all political prisoners—together with potential cadres drawn from the nonpolitical prisoner population. The last-mentioned level would appear to be the optimum situation; however, the absence of group solidarity within the ranks of political prisoners has thus far limited its practical application.

At all Federal and military prisons, inmates are permitted to subscribe to newspapers and magazines, although the total number of subscriptions may be limited. In general, each inmate may receive one home-town newspaper, one national newspaper, and five periodicals. However, periodicals are sometimes censored for political or sexual content. The degree of censorship varies from institution to institution. At the USDB, the *Village Voice* was prohibited reading matter because prison officials deemed it "lewd and lascivious." At Lewisburg Penitentiary, *Playboy* could be purchased at the commissary. At the USDB, "subversive" periodicals like *Esquire, The Nation, The New Republic,* and *Christianity in Crisis,* were banned. The official justification was that all "political" magazines were banned in the "best interests of the prison population."

However, this restriction did not pertain to *Time, Newsweek, U.S. News and World Report,* and an array of right-wing publications ranging from *National Review* to *Thunderbolt.* All of the USDB-banned publications could be received at Lewisburg Penitentiary. It is therefore difficult to generalize regarding censorship: it is a helter-skelter affair, with the final, decision-making power vested in each chief warden.

Prisoners at Federal institutions may also receive books which must, however, be sent directly from the publisher or a bookstore. Books must be approved by the Education department prior to their being given to the prisoner. The degree of censorship thus exercised varies from institution to institution. It has been our observation that book censorship is more relaxed at prison-farm camps which house political prisoners. Prisoners at the Lewisburg Farm Camp have been receiving books by Marx, Lenin, Trotsky, Fanon, Deutscher, Marcuse and other non-USIA-approved authors. Indeed, at that institution, we are unaware of a single instance where a book was prohibited for political reasons. (We have been reliably informed, however, that so liberal a policy is not uniformly characteristic of most Federal prisons.) Had political prisoners at Lewisburg Farm Camp requested permission to receive books dealing with sexual themes, censorship may have been imposed. It was felt that it was not in our interest to do battle over that particular issue.

The USDB provides a singular exception to the rules which we have just outlined. At that institution, only books that are required for correspondence courses or that deal with religious subjects may be mailed to prisoners: the latter variety must be approved by the chaplain's office. When political prisoners attempted to receive books published by Beacon Press (under the auspices of the Uni-

tarian-Universalist Association), many of them were rejected. We were never able to convince the chaplain that
Herbert Marcuse had something relevant to say about con-
temporary religious values. Some theologians would un-
questionably take issue with the standards of the military
chaplains; however, religious militarists have never, to our
knowledge, been part of the ecclesiastical vanguard.*

We suggest that one compile for himself a reading list
prior to entering prison. One might ask a friend or relative
to send a book or two a week from that list. Paperbacks
are preferred, for several reasons; for one thing, they are
easier to carry inconspicuously to work details; for another, books have a high mortality rate in prison. We all
tend to lend books to those who express an interest in
them; however, the rate of return falls far short of one
hundred per cent. Naturally, one can always add or sub-
tract from the original reading list by so advising one's
correspondent. Some political prisoners receive a grab bag
of unrequested books from their correspondents. Experience has taught us that this is an inefficient as well as an
uneconomical way to receive books. It is far better to inform correspondents as to which books one explicitly
wants.

As we have already suggested, another source of learning may be discovered in intergroup and interpersonal
discussions among political prisoners. These latter come
from a variety of social, cultural, political, and academic
backgrounds and these enable them to discuss intelligently
a wide range of subjects. At various times the authors
have spoken about such diverse topics as theology, behavioral psychology, sociology, farming, handwriting analysis, theater, cinema, etc. Subjects relating to politics,

---

* As of summer 1970, a variety of books could be sent to inmates at the
USDB.

such as violence vs. nonviolence, anarchism, history, economic theory, socialism and Marxism, and so on may be endlessly debated and thrashed out.

Not to be overlooked in this process of self-education is the contact prison life affords with nonpolitical inmates. One will find himself living in close proximity to people who have a rich diversiy of backgrounds and life styles. Many political prisoners have led a sheltered and culturally deprived life. Almost any black or hill-country or Puerto Rican prisoner can teach one more about the "culture of poverty" than any book. Nor is it beside the point for the political prisoner to know something about what motivates middle-class men to commit so-called "white collar crimes."

It must be said, however, that we have noticed a certain ambivalence in self-educating discussions with other prisoners. In a sense, one will never be closer to nor have as much time to talk with so many very different personalities. Both groups, however, are too close together and mutually intrude upon each other's privacy. Frank conversations are feared, and both groups tend to turn in upon themselves for defensive purposes. As a consequence, superficial banalities, boredom, and small talk predominate. Nonetheless, true understanding can—and does—break through. The breakthrough is facilitated when political prisoners are able to suppress their own prejudices and preconceptions.

Lastly, contact with prison authorities provides an education unto itself. Many a political prisoner has learned to differentiate friend from foe, and ally from enemy, through his dealings with his captors, the prison administration. We have seen a goodly number of political prisoners completely alter their perspective as a result of this inescapable conflict.

In a sense, then, although the prisoner is amputated from society, he is more a part of it than he ever was prior to his incarceration; for prisons are the bowels of every society. The prisoner is on the inside looking out and this view gives him a new, different, and in many respects a more accurate and faithful rendition of the outside world.

It is our belief that future political prisoners must strive to organize their learning in prison and that they must do so as part of a political cadre. As of now, although prison can offer a learning experience, the self-education which forms its mainstay is haphazard and random. What is clearly needed is an on-going, disciplined, self-educational process into which newcomers can readily be accommodated.

(The following addendum is by David Miller.)

At Allenwood, prior to fall, a ritual takes place that engulfs each succeeding group of political prisoners. We excited ourselves preparing a list of subjects and teachers for a fall-and-winter program of college-level evening classes.

We met with the Education Director. I offered to teach Introductory Sociology, another volunteered for American History, someone else for Physics, others for Black Studies, an English literature course, etc. An assortment of ten different courses with proposed instructors was offered and printed in the camp newspaper. Inmates were to indicate by "cop-outs" (request slips) to the Education Director what courses they were interested in; then the several most requested courses would be assigned a time and place in one of three small rooms in the dilapidated Education Building. The Director gave us a lick and a promise about books and course material, but we started out strongly and enthusiastically anyway. I began my first class with an outdated Introductory Sociology book borrowed from a Muslim. There were ten or twelve inmates in my class, and the other classes were well attended too. I told my students that the Education Director was looking for books over at the wall (inside the penitentiary) and that if he didn't find any, he would buy a few: we went on like this for a couple of weeks, as did the other classes. We made do with what we had. Then someone said that this was a general pattern: everyone starts out with great ideas and plans, but the books and course materials never show up. There might be two or three books to circulate among ten or twelve students. Those most easily discouraged drop out quickly, and in a month or two the classes are down to two or three regular students each. If the instructor is someone—like myself—who isn't an instructor in the first place, he also becomes discouraged at not being able to hold the interest of his students for lack of good material to give them. After four months there might be one or two classes left out of the original group. The lack of materials, adequate classroom space, privacy to read and study, variety in the prison setting— to reduce tension and increase the ability to concentrate— and a history of scholastic failure for many inmates: all these combined to doom our well-intentioned efforts. Until next year, that is.

At Allenwood, a development that held some hope for us was that four Cornell professors started coming down once every two weeks. (I'm told that permission for this has recently been revoked.) One of them was Doug Dowd, the radical economist. With these men we got the books we needed on time, and they were also well-prepared and qualified instructors. Transportation, however, was a prob-

lem for them: the trip from Cornell took two hours one
way and snow kept them away for several weeks at a time.

While at Lewisburg, I took one college-seminar course
inside the wall. There were no classes at the farm camp
but one could sign up for the classes offered at the wall
and be taken there at the proper time. Two or three Bucknell professors held evening classes during the week. I
took a course in the Philosophy of Religion, which met
every other Saturday morning for three hours and was
taught by a Bucknell professor. It was on a freshman or
sophomore level but we brought our varied backgrounds
to it. We read from Paul Tillich, Freud, Marx, and Camus:
except for Tillich I enjoyed the reading and discussion.
Camus has some beautiful passages in *The Plague* about
the feelings and fantasies of the exiled people of Oran;
the inmates really dug them, but they seemed to pass over
the head of the professor.

Back at the farm camp, Howard, Donald, and I read
The Guardian, Monthly Review, The New York Times,
and assorted books, and had long or short discussions
about what we'd read. Howard and Don read more than
I; Don, in fact, spent nearly all of his leisure time—apart
from playing Scrabble and handball—stretched out on his
bunk reading. A black political prisoner at the farm camp
did a great deal of work bringing books and periodicals
around to the brothers and getting them to read.

Chapter 10   MEDICAL CARE

All Federal and military prisons provide medical and dental care for their inmates. In military prisons, these services are provided by active-duty, officer-physicians; whereas in Federal prisons Public Health Service (PHS) physicians are employed.

The prisoner does not usually have direct access to the physician. In most, if not all, Federal prisons the inmate must first present his complaint to a Medical Technical Assistant (MTA) and if, upon the judgment of the MTA, the complaint is legitimate and serious enough he will arrange for the inmate to see the doctor. The MTA's are not physicians, and their only job qualifications are a high-school diploma and minimal medical training—less training, in fact, than that required of a practical nurse. As a group, although there may be exceptions, their laziness is exceeded only by their incompetence. Moreover, in many prisons the inmate must obtain permission from either the domicile hack or the detail supervisor before being permitted to see even the MTA—and if the MTA has little medical training, guards and job overseers have none at all.

Once a prisoner has permission to visit the doctor, he can expect a several-hour wait in the clinic before he finally sees him. The treatment ultimately given varies from fair to good. Most prison physicians have completed only a year of internship, and, perhaps in exceptional cases, a year or two of resident specialty-training. The problem, however, is not so much their lack of experience or technical know-how as it is their uninspired, disinterested, almost lackadaisical approach to the health needs of the prison population.

The reasons for this attitude are not hard to find. Most military physicians dislike military service and impatiently await their discharge date, while in Federal prisons, most PHS physicians are draft dodgers who view their duty as a necessary evil, to be endured in order to escape the clutches of the military. Finally, many in-prison medical problems have an emotional basis and prison physicians are temperamentally ill-equipped to relate to these underlying causative factors. It takes time and a great deal of patience to do so, and as one prison doctor said, "Look man, I just don't give a damn about prisoners. I'm also in prison and only want out." This neglectful attitude toward prisoners' medical problems is reinforced because the oppressiveness and dullness of prison life foster the development of chronic complainers, whose motive in seeking medical care is to avoid work or to obtain stimulants, tranquilizers, sedatives, and the like. The clinic offers prisoners a "change of pace" and avenues of psychological escape. These inmate attitudes also reflect a health problem which prison physicians are incapable of understanding, let alone being able to relate to. Ultimately, the prisoner who is really ill must cope with the universal insensitivity of both his fellow prisoners and doctors when, as is commonly acknowledged, he is most in need of their emotional support.

A backward glance at some of the activities of the medical section at the USDB might help to throw the practice of prison medicine into sharper relief. At the USDB, most routine blood tests and urine tests were never actually run but specimens were, instead, thrown down the laboratory sink while fictitious results were concocted and recorded in the patients' charts; routine chest X rays were not always read but were recorded as "negative" anyway; kitchen workers were supposed to obtain medical clearance before starting on the job—the clearance was given but the workers were never examined; prisoners who were to be sent to disciplinary segregation were supposed to be examined by a physician to determine whether they were able to withstand a restricted diet. These exams were rarely performed but the physicians dutifully filled out the required forms. And so it went. . . .

But prison medicine in Federal institutions is not all bad; it is good enough to keep the inmate alive. If a prisoner is seriously ill, the prison doctor can—and does—call in outside consultants and specialists. The pharmacies are adequate, and if they are tightly controlled and the physician parsimoniously dispenses medication, this is generally the result of the prison officials' fear that prison "pill addicts" might take advantage of a more liberal policy.

Dental care seems, overall, to be a notch better than medical care, probably because all that is demanded of dentists is technical excellence. However, prison dental clinics are understaffed and the wait for a dental appointment sometimes takes from six to twelve months.

Political prisoners are often given an opportunity to work in prison clinics and hospitals. Such assignments might include clerical work, orderly services, and, in some cases, the opportunity to receive valuable training as a laboratory or dental technician. As prison jobs go, one can do much worse; prison medical work can be fairly rewarding and is worthy of consideration. One word of caution is in order: prisoners will ask medical workers for pills of all varieties. Even if medication is accessible, political prisoners should not honor such requests.

One last point must be raised before we take leave of this subject. Prisoners are a prime source of supply for "human guinea pigs" for medical research and experimentation. At several Federal prisons the PHS recruits subjects for various medical-research projects. The military utilizes prisoners for the same purpose. Although there have been a very small number of exceptions, the overwhelming majority of political prisoners have refused to "volunteer" for these projects. Still, because a few political prisoners have offered their bodies and minds, and because the issue affects the general inmate population, the question of medical research and prison "volunteers" should be examined in closer detail.

In Federal prisons, any inmate who "volunteers" to act as a human guinea pig receives rewards from the PHS. Such rewards might include a few extra days' good time (in general, three to ten days are offered), a small cash payment, one or two weeks' reprieve from the prison routine at a PHS hospital, and a notation in his personal prison record to the effect that he has offered his services for the cause of humanity and medical research (sometimes, but not always, one and the same). But the extra good time can be, and sometimes is, later taken away at the discretion of prison officials. The cash payment is usually a nominal sum, about twenty-five dollars. Further, the notation in the prison record carries little weight with parole boards and the tacit promise of an early release is rarely fulfilled.

It is true that no prisoner can be compelled to offer himself to medical research. But then, the prisoner— by virtue of his dependency and vulnerability as a captured party—is unusually susceptible to the blandishments of the researchers and the encouragement of prison officials. He is being bribed, and the largest part of the bribe consists of a few moments of relief from the tedium of prison, together with the unspoken promise of an early release. In truth, the prisoner is in no position to serve as a free *volunteer* precisely because he is not a free *man*.

All medical research carries with it some risk and it should be noted that many eminent scientists have warned that no research should be performed on quasi-volunteers —such as prisoners. This is especially so if the research project does not directly pertain, as it does not in most prison studies, to the health needs of the subject. If these qualifications are not heeded, any risk, however slight, is too great to be ethically justified. It should be stressed that many research projects are ill-conceived and poorly executed. The mystique of the medical researcher has beclouded the fact that only a very small number of research projects yield findings which result in the betterment of mankind. On the contrary, most projects are undertaken for the professional and academic self-aggrandizement of the researcher himself—whose professional star shines ever brighter with each new article he is able to publish in a scientific journal. This is not to suggest that some researchers are not genuinely dedicated and altruistic, but to stress that not every expression of scientific wisdom and benevolence ought be taken at face value.

Certainly, in a prison situation in which prisoners have traditionally suffered at the hands of sometimes overzealous researchers, the political prisoner ought to be conversant with the negative connotations of medical research and should be willing and able to disseminate his knowledge to the general inmate population. When overt abuses occur, he ought to advise outside individuals of the circumstances, so that they may demand the curtailment of the abuses.

Chapter 11   PSYCHIATRY

Prison psychotherapy encompasses individual (or group) therapy and related testing procedures under the guidance of a psychiatrist, clinical psychologist, or social worker. Broadly speaking, fellowships like Alcoholics Anonymous (AA) and Narcotics Anonymous (NA) should be included, although Mental Hygiene Clinic (MHC) personnel may or may not make their services available to the weekly meetings of these largely self-help-oriented groups. Since political prisoners are not likely to avail themselves of the services of either AA or NA we shall confine our attention to the relationship between the political prisoner and MHC personnel.

In a few prisons every inmate receives an initial psychiatric interview and is re-interviewed once a year thereafter—generally shortly before the yearly parole hearings. This is the procedure followed at the USDB, but it is not adhered to in most Federal prisons, some of which do not even employ a psychiatrist. In most prisons each incoming prisoner is asked to take a written psychological test, usually the Minnesota Multiphasic Personality Inventory (MMPI), or some variation thereof. This test, as its title implies, provides the MHC staff with an overall assessment of the testee's psychological make-up and personality and it is also used statistically in various psychological studies in which inmates are employed as investigatory subjects. Prison authorities, though reluctant to make the admission, cannot compel a prisoner to take the test: any attempt to do so would invalidate it. In our limited experience, refusal to submit to the testing procedure resulted in no punitive action. If, however, punitive action were threatened an inmate could evade the punishment and still resist the testing program by taking the exam but intentionally sabotaging the answers. Since these tests employ a multiple-choice format this could easily be done by merely selecting the answers at random.

In those institutions, and they are in the majority, where psychiatric interviews are not mandatory, the political prisoner may come into contact with the MHC either by choice or because, for one reason or another, prison authorities demand a psychiatric evaluation. Obviously, there is no reason to believe that political prisoners are singularly free from mental-health problems; if such difficulties exist—or arise—the inmate is well advised to seek the help of the MHC. On the other hand, it should be pointed out that political prisoners, and in particular, those among them who resist prison authority, are often advised to seek psychiatric assistance although they suffer no psychiatric maladies. This practice is reminiscent of the state of affairs which not long ago prevailed in the USSR, and probably still does, whereby the mere act of resisting in and of itself was proof of mental instability. Then too, it may be noted that psychiatrists, psychologists, and social workers often have an almost morbid and voyeuristic—or guilt-provoked—longing to meet with political prisoners and therefore, of their own accord, request to interview them.

Bitter experience has taught us that in the absence of a truly compelling need, political prisoners are wise to refrain from associating with any of the activities—or the personnel—of the Mental Hygiene Clinic. Mental Hygiene Clinic personnel are employed by the prison system which provides them with a salary, office space, equipment, housing facilities, and last, but by no means least, a set of rules and regulations that severely compromise their professional competence and integrity.

Where there is no actual psychopathology present, Mental Hygiene Clinic personnel are rarely in a position to significantly help the political prisoner. To do so almost always, in the final analysis, necessitates that they jeopardize their own privileged position and well-being. When mental-hygiene workers do offer help it is of the most trivial nature, e.g., one psychiatrist attempted to befriend one of the authors [H.L.], by offering to allow him to read his copies of *Ramparts* magazine. (The offer was declined.)

More often than not, prison mental-health workers are detrimental to the welfare of the political prisoner. For example, psychiatrists often affix a diagnostic label to the political prisoner—especially to the prison resister. Thus one may be labeled a "passive-aggressive" or "immature" personality. This labeling device—though more sophisticated—is no different in kind from the attempt of other prison authorities to characterize political prisoners as "kooks and malcontents." The psychiatric label has a double edge: it may socially isolate the political prisoner and encourage his castigation by the general inmate population; and it may introduce an element of doubt into his mind concerning the logic and motivations of his political position. In general, the psychiatrist functions in order to "pacify" the prison resister. He is told that he should "adjust" to prison and assured that the psychiatrist will assist him in this endeavor. We feel that each political prisoner must decide for himself whether it is best to "adjust" to, or resist, prison authority. If his choice is the latter, he ought to steer clear of the Mental Hygiene Clinic.

Other problems inherent in the relationship between political prisoners and the Mental Hygiene Clinic should be mentioned. The findings and conclusions of the psychiatrist and the results of psychological testing become a part of the prisoner's record. In the military, privileged communication with a psychiatrist (or for that matter with any physician) is nonexistent. The situation with reference to the Federal prison system is less clearly defined but it is reasonable to assume that privileged communication is nonexistent here as well. Recently, for example, political opinions expressed at a group-therapy session at Lewisburg Farm Camp found their way back—via the loose-tongued psychiatrist—to the general inmate population and presumably to the prison administration. While this specific indiscretion was of little moment, other situations may be envisioned where such "slips" could be very harmful. It might be disastrous for a political prisoner who intends to pursue a public career to confide potentially embarrassing personal details about himself in an unprivileged psychiatric interview. This concern is more than a matter of prison paranoia. Not long ago *The New York Times* reported the conclusions of an army psychiatric interview made ten years earlier with a black man, Ahmed Evans, who allegedly ambushed and killed several Cleveland policemen. Where did the newspaper obtain this damaging and prejudicial information? More recently, a book review of Mark Lane's *Conversations with Americans*, appeared in *The New York Times*. In an attempt to discredit the book, the reviewer described one of the GI interviewees as a homosexual and a narcotics user. No mention had been made of this in the book itself. The GI, who was confined in a stockade, told a military psychiatrist this information in order to obtain his release from confinement.

Frequently, the Mental Hygiene Clinic cooperates with prison officials in identifying "troublemakers." At the USDB, the Mental Hygiene Clinic was instrumental, time after time, in selecting "troublemakers" for transfer to other, sometimes tougher, Federal prisons. Thus the Clinic is seen to function hand in glove with the authorities. To confide in the prison psychiatrist is, essentially, to confide in the chief warden; while in principle, candor is an admirable trait, it is, in prison, often unwise. It should be recalled that in prison snitching is a "capital offense," and it makes no practical difference whether the "'dime is dropped" directly to a prison official or indirectly, to this same official, via the psychiatrist.

In addition to directly reporting "troublemakers" to prison authorities, the Mental Hygiene Clinic is sometimes called upon to contribute in other ways to the prison pacification program. Thus, at the USDB, one of the authors [H.L.] discovered to his surprise that he was not permitted to receive the book, *Black Rage*, after psychiatrists were asked by prison authorities to pass judgment on the medical merits of the book. (Dr. Levy was permitted to receive medical books.) Regardless of the general popularity of *Black Rage*, it was written by two black psychiatrists, it has been extensively reviewed in medical journals, and it is, without question, a medical book. The psychiatrists thought otherwise and, in effect, exercised political censorship in denying the book to the inmate.

Mental Hygiene Clinics are utilized by the Federal Bureau of Prisons as justification for its claim that prisons are rehabilitative. In truth, prison psychotherapy is superficial and likely to prove of no lasting benefit to most patients. Mental Hygiene Clinics simply become a part of the penal system's public-relations arsenal and serve to buttress and stabilize these institutions. Many political prisoners are beginning to have second thoughts about cooperating with this aspect of their incarceration.

Finally, Mental Hygiene Clinic personnel employ a "soft-sell" technique. These mental-health technicians will not berate or chastise inmates and it is only rarely, and with great reluctance, that they will punish them. This deceptive benevolence—deceptive because these people serve the interests of the institution first and of the inmates only incidentally—has earned for these technicians the opprobrious designation, "new custodians." "New," not because they pursue aims that are different from the old but only because the carrot has been found to be more effective in enforcing discipline than the stick. In point of fact, both new and old custodians are still, fundamentally, cops. And in the light of the "new custodians'" success in pacifying potential "'agitators and troublemakers," even the old custodians are adapting the new behavioristic techniques. The associate warden of Lewisburg Federal Penitentiary recently assured a political-prisoner resister that he was a "professional behavioral scientist." True enough: and food for thought.

Chapter 12 PUNISHMENT

One would think that imprisonment is punishment enough, and it is. But to preserve order, and to effectively administer the institution, there of necessity emerges a complicated pattern of reward and punishment. The punishments, to a large degree, are simply the absence of rewards for good behavior. It appears that the basis of prison operation is that anything given to an inmate beyond keeping him in twenty-four-hour lockup is a privilege contingent upon his behavior. The fact that the great majority of inmates is not under such a lockup is an indication of the manipulative effectiveness of the cards the administration holds.

Quite naturally, the administration hopes that every inmate will go along with the prison program. The inmate, it is hoped, will report to work on time, do a job to the satisfaction of the detail supervisor, respect count time, give the "proper" courteous respect to staff members, keep out of fights, keep his living area and person in a fashion worthy of presentation to the staff, and abide by the multitude of other rules, regulations, and procedures that make up prison life. Needless to say, the enforcement of the prison routine, and the "'adjustment" of the inmates to the prison program is a major administrative problem. Indeed, after a period of imprisonment it becomes apparent that the technique of behavior manipulation is the only real problem and, hence, concern of the prison administrators: not the welfare of the inmate, not the exalted ideals of rehabilitation, not the social changes so drastically needed in society, not concern over the grossly unjust imprisonment of their captives and the terrible effect that prison has on them and on society. None of these considerations are of any importance to the administrators. Their concern lies in making their job as easy as possible—and their job is to see that every inmate does his time and completes his sentence with the least possible friction. That way there is less pain all around. To achieve that end each prisoner is asked to "join the team." But the facts of imprisonment do not allow the painless way to prevail. To inflict pain when the occasion demands, the prison administration makes use of the following devices: new prosecution in Federal court for something which allegedly occurred within the prison; revocation of statutory and/or earned good time; loss of reasonable chance of parole; confinement to the "hole," i.e., the segregation unit; loss of quarters, i.e., being sent back to less favorable quarters, such as the jungle; return from the farm to the penitentiary; confinement to quarters during recreation periods—no TV, movies or yard time; five-hour extra-duty assignments; job transfer; transfer to another institution; transfer to Springfield for psychiatric reasons; beatings, tear gassing and Macing by the prison goon squad; and an assortment of other harassments.

It often happens that an inmate can become marked for harassment. If an inmate (or group of inmates) "causes trouble" the staff is quite capable of returning the favor by being tougher with the presumed source of the trouble: it is a philosophy of give and take. But it is a give-and-take situation in which the prisoners are at an unspeakable disadvantage.

A man on whom the prison staff looks with disfavor can be kicked around or given the run-around in all departments of the prison: on his job, in the education department, in the visiting procedures, medical treatment, mental hygiene clinic, etc. There are many ways to direct or mold a man's will and, if need be, eventually to break it. Time and most other resources are on their side, not the prisoner's.

From the warden's office down to the lowliest custodial official, there is a constant stream of advice to "make it easy on yourself," "think of your chance for parole," "think of your family." But if perchance you do not think of these things from the approved and sanctioned point of view of the prison authorities, they will be as ruthless as the situation demands. All dissidence is eyed as a threat to the authority of the administration.

Good time comes in two varieties, statutory good time and earned good time. Statutory good time is awarded by law in an ascending scale depending on length of sentence. A thirty-month sentence entitles the holder to six months' statutory good time lopped off his sentence. A sixty-month sentence would give the inmate something over double the six months provided for the thirty-month sentence. Earned good time is further divided into industrial good time, camp good time, and meritorious good time. Industrial good time is earned by working in prison industries and will range from two to five days a month, again depending on length of sentence. Camp good time is awarded to all inmates at the minimum-security farm camps starting at three days a month and rising to five days a month after one year. Meritorious good time is a special bonus (usually from three to thirty days) for an inmate who may have worked seven days a week for a year or for an inmate who may have ratted on a fellow inmate's escape plan. But what the warden hath given, the warden can taketh away. The good-time forfeiture board can take any or all of an inmate's statutory and/or earned good time. It is constantly threatened and frequently done.

A description of the good-time forfeiture board significantly reveals the power and the arbitrary latitude of decision the administration possesses over the inmates. The good-time forfeiture board meets one or two days a month and handles the entire month's cases in this time. The board is duly constituted *within prison procedures* as a trial board governing the revocation of all forms of good time that may result from a conviction of an institutional infraction. It consists of several prison officials, a stenographer, and the accused inmate.

The proceeding is convened and the accused inmate read a charge and asked if he understands it. He is advised that he will be given a chance to read something into the record later on, but that he does not have to say anything if he chooses not to. An assortment of memos from staff members purporting to give factual evidence and substantiation to the charge are read. Then the board members are free to question the accused after which the latter can speak for the record. After that, if there is nothing to be added by the board members, the proceeding is concluded and the board informs the inmate that he will be advised of the verdict. But the verdict is well-known to the accused, and is, in fact, a foregone conclusion. The defendant is not allowed to be represented by counsel; he is not permitted to bring witnesses to testify in his behalf; he is not permitted to cross-examine those staff members who drew up the reports on him, because they are not present; he is given no indication concerning the mechanics of appeal—if any. It is simply a matter of his word against that of the staff and there is no question about whose will carry the day.

Let us cite an example from a military prison, the United States Disciplinary Barracks. There a Discipline & Adjustment (D&A) Board meets weekdays to "try" inmates who have been accused of violations of institutional rules.

A political prisoner [H.L.] was called before this board because it was alleged that he had sent contraband through the mail to his lawyer. The board was particularly upset over some material relating to press censorship at the institution. The inmate brought to the board's attention that the material in question was not contraband because he was preparing to challenge legally the prerogatives of the prison's censors and that, moreover, the institution had no right to determine what was and was not proper areas of concern between a client and his attorney. He also pointed out that in order to discover the alleged contraband in the first place, the officials of the USDB must have opened his privileged communication to and from his lawyer and that this was in clear and unequivocal violation of the institution's own written rules and regulations. Notwithstanding, he was summarily sentenced to an indeterminate stay in the hole. He was not, but could have been, deprived of all or part of his good time as well.

The good-time forfeiture boards in the Federal system and the Disciplinary and Adjustment boards in the military are shocking examples of violation of judicial due process. The power which these pseudo-judicial boards hold to deprive prisoners of their good time is awesome. To deprive a man of months and even years of good time is equivalent to adding months and years to his sentence. When a judge sentences a man to a five-year prison term, he expects that the man will be released in about three years if he is not paroled even earlier. But if a man violates a trivial institution rule, a board consisting of prison officials and ultimately responsible only to the chief warden can, in effect, add two years to the man's sentence merely by revoking his good time. That one man, the warden, should be vested with so much power—power uncontrolled by judicial restraint—is an abomination.

The prospect of losing good time haunts every inmate. And the institution's power over good time makes it a valuable pawn in the manipulative game. What makes the situation more difficult is the quasi-legal status afforded forfeiture boards by the Federal courts. The courts have ruled that a prisoner cannot be tried by both a Federal court and the prison for the same offense: it must be one or the other. Thus, if an inmate is tried for possession of narcotics in prison and loses some good time, he cannot then be hauled into Federal court and tried again. But by the same token, Federal courts have, by and large, adopted a "hands off" policy with respect to the arbitrary decisions of prison disciplinary boards. The courts are extremely reluctant to review in-prison disciplinary procedures, the result being that these procedures are never scrutinized by independent judicial bodies.

Since a prisoner's job detail (*see* "Work") is of considerable importance to him from several points of view, the absolute power of the administration to determine job assignments represents another powerfully effective coercive tool. One's behavior and work attitude are prime factors in where an inmate will end up. Any infraction on or off the job can cause him to be busted from a comparatively good job to a worse one. One could, for example, have a sweet job in the education department and then find oneself washing pots in the dish room; or one can go from an office clerk to mopping hallways. The industrial job situation is especially revealing. Many men inside the walls prefer to work in industry for the extra earned good time, as well as for the money which can be used for commissary, sent home, or saved until their release date. Thus, the possibility of being busted from an industrial job becomes an effective threat, especially for the poor prisoner.

The threat of being transferred from one institution to another is an even more effective tool in the prison administrator's battle with those prisoners, political and otherwise, who refuse to become "adjusted." The descriptive term is the "prison merry-go-round." It is not unusual for a man doing a bit of, let us say, five to ten years to be familiar with four or five institutions. Just as job security in prison is absent, residence security is, as well. There may be any number of reasons for transferring men. For instance, there are always a number of men who constantly botch their jobs, or who cannot get along with other prisoners. In order to avoid trouble, the administration must keep these men moving. Again, the power of transfer is used to great advantage in breaking up coalitions that threaten the institution. Individuals within groups of "troublemakers" are sent traveling in different directions. This may happen to political and non-political prisoners alike. Not long ago at Lewisburg Penitentiary a group of prisoners in one of the industrial plants went on strike. Several spokesmen for the group were invited to air their grievances before the administration. The officials listened, said nothing, and within a few days all of the spokesmen were transferred out of the institution and the strike was broken.

The effectiveness of transfer in avoiding trouble and breaking resistance is too apparent to require elaboration. But one of its concomitants is the disorientation of the inmate who has been transferred. To begin with, he will be transferred cross-country by bus, with stopovers at several county and Federal jails, the entire trip taking four to six weeks. Once he has arrived at his final destination he can expect that it will take anywhere from three to six months to acquaint himself with and relate to his new

prison community: he must make new friends and size up
the new joint. All of this takes time.

We knew of one black political prisoner, a key organizer for the Student National Coordinating Committee
(SNCC), who, during one six-month stretch in Federal
prison never spent more than a month at any one institution. He was transferred from place to place not because
he broke prison regulations but rather because prison officials, well aware of his reputation, were fearful that he
might organize the black inmates.

The goon squad is the instrument of actual physical oppression. They may, at times, wield clubs, but never carry
any firearms on their persons. Except for times of actual
riot, no member of the staff has firearms on his person.
The nearest gun toters are the guards in the towers. In the
Lewisburg complex (the penitentiary, farm camp, and Allenwood), all that needs be done for a guard to get some
action is to pick up one of the many inter-institution
phones, dial 222, and holler "Help." Within a few minutes
ten, fifteen, or forty hacks are on the spot to beat the culprit into submission and to take him to the hole. The extent
of the beating depends on the circumstances. The beating
on the way to the hole is less severe if the trouble is a matter of a fight between inmates. It is much more severe if
an inmate were beating a hack.

The tenor of a goon-squad encounter can be shown by
the following example. A hack called the goon squad after
an inmate seemingly threatened to become violent when
told to get off a ping-pong table he was lying on. The goon
squad burst upon the scene and without any hesitation
proceeded to lay low an innocent bystander. It was a man
who had just come in and was standing nearby with his
blanket and bed linen in his arms.

Beatings are somewhat less likely to be the fate of dissident political prisoners if only because prison officials are terrified of the adverse publicity which might ensue after such a confrontation. Nevertheless, in the heat of the moment, a prisoner's "notoriety" may fail to protect him from the goon squad. Of course, the goon squad is not the ultimate force. Even the rifle-bearing tower sharpshooters are not final. All prisoners know that nothing short of massive military might would be unleashed against them should they have the collective gall not to appreciate their situation.

Institutions holding prisoners for long stays are a relatively new phenomena. They are a response to the public's repugnance with and repudiation of methods of corporal punishment (hanging, torture, execution, etc.) which held sway for many years and which, while they were brutal, did have the "advantage" of rapid termination. Further, penal methods in the United States have shown a steady decline in physical violence. This trend is most marked in the Federal penal system. Federal prisons exhibit a decided turn toward more "progressive" methods, a more "professional" approach. This does not mean that prisons are less brutal today than in times past. What has happened is that physical tools have been replaced by psychological tools. The brutality of the latter are less visible but in terms of accomplishment they are, because of their very effectiveness in reducing men to a state of total, childlike dependency, perhaps even more brutal. Furthermore, there has been no loss in the prison administration's arsenal: there has been a gain. The physical force is not absent, it is only kept out of sight and in reserve. Parole, good time, halfway houses, farm camps, etc., have simply nudged physical force gently into the dark corners and recesses of the prison system.

Chapter 13   RATS AND SNITCHES

Every new prisoner must learn to appreciate three things concerning rats and snitches in prison. The first is how to recognize those inmates most likely to be snitches; the second is to realize that one is going to have to live in close personal contact with them; the third is to see how, and the extent to which, the administration uses them.

Don't take anyone in prison at face value. The most militant-looking and tough-rapping prisoner may be the biggest snitch. Although it is not always true, a lot of snitches have the best jobs in each institution: they are the closest to the seat of power and they have "the ear of the king," so to speak. A likely snitch can also be spotted by the amount of time he got for a particular crime, if the sentence is much less than it should normally be. For instance, a first bust for selling heroin nets you a "pound" (five years). If a man comes in with two years for dope, one can guess that he ratted someone out in court. If a man comes in with two or three years for bank robbery or post-office robbery, and his partners got fifteen or twenty, it's a good bet that his testimony in court "buried" them. In the end, however, one has to rely on a few inmates whose integrity one trusts to point out the snitches; one must also rely on his own experience.

Snitches are despised, but contrary to the movies, the majority of them are not bumped off once they become known; they remain very much alive and kicking. A good number of them may be moved from the penitentiary to the farm camp for safer keeping, but even inside the wall there are plenty of them. Though some are in serious danger of being hurt, most inmates are realistic enough not to want to try and beat a murder charge—even if they would like to kill someone who snitched on them. The result is that snitches go on living: you might end up sleeping right next to one, in which case, at least a few pleasantries have to be exchanged once in awhile, even though this may be repugnant. If you aren't ready to "call him out," then you have to live with him. It certainly isn't wise to hang out with a snitch but in the closeness of prison life one finds it necessary to accept the fact that they are almost ever present.

Any time that one inmate snitches on another, that fact is entered in the former's record: there is then a permanent notation of that inmate's cooperation with the authorities. The inmate who has once snitched will be used by prison officials as often as they need him; they know that he will snitch again if they hold something over his head—parole, good time, a new charge, or a few privileges. We recall that one well-known snitch at the farm camp was "given" a passive homosexual: the latter was allowed to move into his room.

Within the "ground rules," and depending on what they think they can get away with, prison officials will try to get any inmate to snitch. The sad fact is that there are plenty of inmates ready to cut your throat for the price of a few extra good days, or a telephone call—certainly for a parole. You had better believe that there are cutthroats in the penitentiary, made that way by a cutthroat society. The administration encourages them and uses them ruthlessly. They are not the primary enemy but be wary: not paranoid, but wary.

—DAVID MILLER

Chapter 14   VIOLENCE

Violence in prison is a serious and constant threat that all prisoners must live with. There are two kinds of violence, that between inmate and inmate, and that between staff and inmate. We should preface this chapter by saying that both authors—as well as most other political prisoners—have done their entire bits without one physical fight. But although we may have avoided fighting, the fear and the ever present threat of violence was unavoidable. In some ways, the constant state of preparedness was harder on our minds and bodies than actual physical violence might have been.

The amount of prison violence would be hard to guess: perhaps it is no greater than it is in any other situation—especially in our cities. There might be several murders and stabbings a year, along with several fights every few weeks. But the near misses, the verbal fights, the times that tremendous urges toward violence are suppressed by sheer will power—these would be impossible to tabulate. One of the most amazing things about prison is the seemingly successful suppression of enormous frustrations and destructive urges: it is a very unhealthy but very necessary suppression. No inmate can afford to go around fighting all the time if he wants to survive. He who does has the label "no understanding" applied to him.

There is no real way in prison to work out one's frustrations and anger. Lifting weights, running track, playing handball or other sports, or even working hard cannot take care of the need for relieving bottled-up emotions. The better part of these emotions must be swallowed whole. This phenomenon strikes us as being one of the primary

destructive aspects of prison in terms of warping and em-
bittering inmates' personalities. The huge reservoir of suppressed aggression among prisoners must find its way out
at some time and that time is usually when they are free
again. Prisoners get on one another's nerves. Even if
one likes some of his fellows, they are ever present—the
lack of privacy grates at the insides month after month,
year after year. The inmate would like to shout and kick
and beat someone's head in, but he can't do that. He
doesn't want to get hurt and he doesn't want to lose good
time or parole. So he swallows again and tries to find something to do.

There is a definite mentality concerning personal violence dominant among the majority of inmates. It is a kind
of combination gangster and cowboy mentality, characteristic of people without power. It is played up by television
and the movies, and is an approach to violence that is individual, romantic, and self-assertive; individual prowess
is more revered than is organized group protection. It is
no wonder that this type of mentality pervades the prisons.
The administration works consciously and continually to
thwart any form of political organization among inmates.
It thus becomes necessary for everyone to protect himself
and this produces a need, on the part of many prisoners, to
over-emphasize themselves as tough guys, as gangsters.

The most violent types are usually young, are charac-
terized as having "no understanding," and are doing no
more than five- or ten-year bits. The older inmates and the
young ones with twenty or thirty years or more are much
less likely to be troublemakers: there is a great difference,
too, between big-mouth bluffers and silent killers. The
novice prisoner will find that the loudest, most boisterous
and obnoxious inmates are the least likely to be killers.
There definitely *are* killers in prison but they don't shout
about it.

A serious problem of some political prisoners is to be taken in by the apparent toughness of loud, flashy inmates. One must learn to be able to take part in a lot of give-and-take horseplay. However, don't engage in too much horseplay; it can become serious. Going too far can be a bad mistake in prison. Above all—stay away from "no understanding" dudes. Stand up for your rights, but don't underestimate anyone and don't back anyone into a corner they can't get out of. We are firmly convinced that size doesn't matter very much in successfully warding off potential trouble. Attitude is what is most important. The majority of inmates does not *want* to fight; if it sees you can't be bluffed, it doesn't matter how small you are; if other prisoners are convinced that you'll fight—whatever your size—they won't bother you, as a rule. ➝

One of the reasons for a lot of the horseplay and semi-serious threats is the same as for much of the homosexual play: to act out and verbalize what one would like to do but can't allow himself to do. Fighting in prison carries heavy sexual overtones. Men say, "I'm going to knock him down and then I'm going to fuck him." One must be aware of the function of all the tough talk and not be afraid of it. The best way to react is in a give-and-take manner—without going overboard. Play the game and learn to know what is serious and what is not.

Many times, inmates will act to break up or cool down fights among other inmates. Mostly, friends will intervene between other friends—this happens most often at the farm camps. When fights break out there, especially on the ball field or in other recreational areas, there will almost certainly be intervention and it will be over quickly. Inmates act to "save" others from being hurt or busted on account of fighting, unless it is known that one of the parties is very unpopular and needs a beating; or if it is obvious that there really is bad blood between the parties.

In the penitentiary there is less intervention because fights are more serious. Most guys step back out of the way when a fight breaks out; it is too dangerous to get involved in trying to stop a fight inside the penitentiary. A small fight can easily lead to a big one, maybe even to a riot.

There are some areas where it is more dangerous to fight than in others. In fact, those who fight in crowded, open areas are punished more by the prison administration than those who fight in small, out-of-the-way places. Technically, if an inmate fights in the dining hall, movie theater, prison yard, or any other area where large numbers of men congregate, he can be charged with inciting to riot, or with inciting to riot to precipitate an escape. The administration doesn't take such incidents lightly.

There is always the danger of riot. It can happen any time and for any seemingly trivial reason. It must be said for prison administrators that they are trained, by years of experience, to see when there is real danger of a riot. There are times when tension is higher than other times; it might be in the summer when everyone is hot and sticky, or it might be in the winter when everyone is inside with no outdoor recreation and the confinement maddening. Everything seems the same, including the laughter, but the tension can be cut with a knife. Once an inmate friend said that an officer told him, "I'm going to show you that I know my job." He then predicted that something would occur before the weekend was over. Sure enough, that weekend a bunch of prisoners tore up the library.

As a final word on prison violence and riots, we might suggest a distinction between what prison administrators call a "riot" and what we call a "rebellion." Many prison "riots" are, in fact, rebellions. The prison administration uses the term riot to suggest an unreasonable attack on prison property and personnel. Prisoners use the term rebellion to indicate that the force used in these cases is reasonably aimed at correcting inhuman conditions. Further, the term riot implies a lack of direction and organization. But it seems apparent that this shoe does not fit recent prison uprisings in New York City and Auburn, New York, and elsewhere.

Chapter 15

The societal tensions and conflicts which affect the nation as a whole likewise affect prison communities. Thus racial strife is duplicated and perhaps even exaggerated in prison. The white prisoner, unlike white Americans on the other side of the prison gate, cannot dissociate himself from the problem by the simple expedient of fleeing to the suburbs; he is trapped and has no place to flee. Close living conditions, such as exist in all prisons, tend to foster petty animosities under the best circumstances. And when there is added to these personal frictions the catalytic agent of racial discord, a highly combustible situation results.

In virtually every prison the proportion of nonwhite to white prisoners is twice that of the general population of the United States. As a rough and unofficial estimate, nonwhite prisoners account for between twenty and twenty-five per cent of the Federal prison population. The usual explanation given is that these figures merely reflect the fact that nonwhite Americans commit more crimes than do white Americans. The explanation misses the point, to wit, that typical white middle- and upper-class crimes are rarely punished (i.e., tax evasion and underhand business dealings), and crimes committed by white middle-class youth are frequently overlooked and never come to trial; furthermore, even when they do, prison sentences are less frequently imposed. Thus, crime statistics which purport to show a racial etiology are more a reflection of a white, racist, bourgeois-oriented law-enforcement and judicial system than they are of actual incidences of criminal activity. Many of the crimes which result in Federal convictions of nonwhites are really nothing more than the business activities of men for whom other avenues of "legitimate" business are closed. (Of course, we do not condone the drug trade in the nonwhite—or for that matter, in the white—community. As these communities become politicized, the curtailment of the activities of pushers will certainly be accorded high priority in any radical program. Nevertheless, we must realize that pushers are merely employing the techniques of capitalism in order to earn enough money to feed their own habits and stomachs.) We find in prison men who have had no choice but to hustle for a living in order to support themselves and their families. Many black prisoners (as well as a very substantial number of white prisoners) are, in effect, doing time for society's crimes.

Once within the walls of the prison, nonwhite—in particular, black—prisoners are discriminated against and come to harbor grievances far beyond those of most other inmates. In most prisons black faces are rarely seen in the front office of the administration building and the number of black guards is disproportionate to the overall racial composition of the prison population; even when blacks are found in custodial positions, they often mete out harsher treatment and punishment to black prisoners and demand that they adhere more strictly and exactingly to the institutions' rules and regulations than do whites. In short, black custodians are often thought of as "Uncle Toms." White officials are usually racists of long standing and deep conviction, and even in those exceptional instances when this may not be the case, these officials have little or no comprehension of the changing dynamics of race relations. For example, at the USDB, black prisoners were often chided—and sometimes punished—for sporting Afro hairstyles. Ostensibly, this was because such styles did not conform to army standards concerning hair length.

A glance at the long hair of many white prisoners would have quickly shattered that "explanation."

Racial slurs and innuendoes are commonplace in prison and black prisoners are often ordered to perform the most menial jobs: in most prisons, black prisoners are likely to make up the bulk of the kitchen brigade and they are also assigned to other undesirable clean-up details. Many fewer black prisoners than whites are placed in "white collar" prison jobs—such as teaching school. These exclusions are, we hasten to add, not total: Federal- and military-prison officials have learned the benefits of adopting a tokenistic approach and use it to maximum public-relations advantage. But at the USDB, black prisoners who were thoroughly qualified to teach school were frequently refused such employment because of their supposed "militancy." Likewise, black prisoners were often denied employment on the writing staff of the prison magazine.

In manipulating black inmates, the prison administration attempts to keep up with the times. Black power, black consciousness, and black culture are very much part of the times. In order to corral what could turn out to be violent expressions of black identity, prison officials have decided to give some "play" to rising black consciousness. Technically, the Muslims have been allowed to exist openly in Federal prisons for some time. But recently, prison officials have approved the creation of black-culture groups. These groups are appearing in state and Federal prisons all across the country. In Lewisburg, just before the authors were released, the ABCD (African Black Cultural Development Society) was started; there was also a Black Literature group that met every week. Here, apparently, was progressive innovation. But as it does every other organization in prison, the administration thoroughly emasculated the black-culture groups. It kept a very close watch on them and would never let things "get out of hand." It planted some of its most notorious snitches within the framework of these groups. Conceivably, someone may have gotten some benefit from these groups, but the administration at Lewisburg is clearly playing games with black inmates with its "commitment" to black culture. The real message from the prison administration to the black inmates was communicated right after a "riot situation" in which several guards were injured by Muslim inmates. In the week that followed that incident about twenty non-Muslim black inmates were rounded up by the administration; they represented some of the most articulate and militant blacks in the penitentiary. Most of them were shipped out to other prisons. A harsh, repressive move like that is where prison officials really are on the race question; they are not interested in black consciousness.

But racism in prison is not confined to officials and guards. White prisoners are, not surprisingly, imbued with the same racial values that characterize white American society as a whole. It is worth considering that for the first and no doubt only time in their lives (excluding military service), Jews and Italians from the East Coast, "hillbillies" from the coal fields of Kentucky and West Virginia, and Protestants from the sprawling suburbs are being forced to live, sleep, and bathe alongside black men from the nation's ghettos and rural communities. Here, then, could seemingly occur the fulfillment—in an admittedly distorted social environment—of the racial integrationists' dream. (In passing, it is of some interest to note that the only places where integration has "worked" has been in mind-killing prisons and body-killing armies.) But this is not yet the case; although white and black prisoners live and coexist in close physical proximity, the mental and social distance between them is as great as the distance between New York and Peking.

Prisoners, especially chronic prisoners, quickly become "con wise." Inmates, both white and black, know that they must coexist, and they adapt to this reality by establishing tenuous and superficial social relationships with one another. Only in the rarest instances do white and black prisoners develop a feeling of kinship with one another: the true hostility which continues to plague the races lurks, barely disguised, immediately beneath the veneer of civility. When, as frequently happens, the tissue-paper amenities are torn asunder, the true situation is exposed and fights, verbal and physical, erupt volcanically. At such times the races are revealed as distinctly separate and hostile camps. The racial mix is extremely volatile and the political prisoner must walk the narrow line between and among the mutually antagonistic camps. On either side of the line there is great danger and the political prisoner is forever on the verge of falling in one direction or the other.

Political prisoners tend to be far less racist than the average white inmate. Therefore, when confronted with evidences of white racism, they have a gnawing desire to attempt to mitigate these expressions of hate. Occasionally, black prisoners encourage these efforts, but for the most part, the more politically conscious black prisoners realize, as do we, the impotence and shortcomings of this approach. The white prisoner will not welcome criticism and he does not feel that he needs advice. He is likely to say something like, "If I need your shit, I'll beat it out of you." Tackling his racism head-on will surely result in rebuff; it will accomplish nothing except, conceivably, the soothing of one's own conscience. We are not suggesting that political prisoners withdraw from the white prison community but we do suggest that if one is concerned with politicizing that community, one begin with issues which immediately address themselves to its self-interest. If political prisoners ever succeed in even partially politicizing white inmates, perhaps the problem of white racism may be broached and prove soluble.

Although it is clear that white political prisoners cannot tackle white racism head-on, we do not mean to suggest that when the subject crops up, as it often does, the white political prisoner should hide his sympathies for the black-liberation movement. The authors have been perfectly candid in talking with white prisoners and have found that our candor in regard to racism and the black struggle has not alienated us from them. But candor and a willingness to put our political beliefs out in the open is not the same thing as attempting to convince a man, through argument, to renounce his racist beliefs. It is our opinion that heated debates cannot succeed in achieving the desired result; instead, it will only create new hostilities which one can well do without.

Often, even prior to the time that he gets his first stinging rebuke from the other white prisoners, the political prisoner may offer his assistance and advice to the black prison community only to receive a rebuff. Although most political prisoners intellectually identify with the growing mood of black militancy, up until now relatively few of them have had any firsthand practice in relating to black militants; as a consequence, they compromise their standing with these people very early in their prison experience. And in prison one's good standing, once lost, may be impossible to retrieve later.

In nearly all prisons, black militancy expresses itself in some or all of the following ways: black prisoners, whenever possible, "segregate" themselves in dining rooms, chapels, and movies; regulations permitting, they attempt to monopolize the TV sets and dictate the programs to be watched; they may try to minimize the participation of white prisoners in athletic events; Afro hairdo's or completely shaved heads are the norms; and black militants display at best, an impatience with white prisoners and, at worst, a derogatory attitude toward them.

This behavior often evokes protests from the novice white political prisoner—as well as from other white prisoners—and these protests, in turn, are greeted by angry tirades and sometimes physical abuse.

Perhaps the most extreme and graphic illustration of in-prison racial animosity is the periodic raping of young white inmates by black prisoners. Certainly not every white inmate is assaulted, nor is every black inmate looking for a "piece of white ass." Indeed, the vast majority of white and black inmates are neither victims nor perpetrators of these atrocious acts. However, the few prisoners who are involved further poison an atmosphere already suffocatingly polluted.

As noted, prison life magnifies and exaggerates race-related political and social forces which are at work throughout the society; the microscopic becomes macroscopic and what is distant is magnified into immediate and discomforting proximity. It should be obvious, but often is not, that these forces have their roots in America's racist past and are nurtured by its racist present. It should be equally obvious that black militancy is a necessary response to years of crushing oppression and enforced submissiveness; it represents an effort to reclaim a lost sense of pride, esteem, and initiative. This movement toward a new assertiveness is politically, socially, and psychologically healthy—in spite of the occasional harmful side effects it may engender. It goes without saying that today's black militancy is a far cry from traditional Christian-pacifist beliefs, hopes, and expectations. Into this turmoil of white racism and black power, the novice white political prisoner is thrust.

Most white political prisoners are justifiably proud of the sacrifices which they have made on behalf of their principles and communities. Although this pride could act as a valuable resource to help the political prisoner survive his months and years of incarceration the commendable traits of quiet, inner pride and confidence unfortunately often manifest themselves outwardly as haughty arrogance. Despite the fact that the black prisoner nurses an underlying respect for the white political prisoner, it is unlikely that he will or can afford to pay the homage which many political prisoners feel is their due. One must consider the black militant's knowledge that the sacrifices made by the white political prisoner are minuscule when compared to those sacrifices which have involuntarily been the lot of the black man from birth. Seen in this light, any demand or expectation on the part of white political prisoners for respect and recognition are likely to be met by black inmates with stony silence and icy indifference. Even if the latter begrudgingly respect the white political prisoner, an overwhelming sense of distrust—and even hatred—for the white man's very freedom to make his voluntary sacrifice discolors and distorts the blacks' judgment and evaluation.

The white political prisoners' relationship to black inmates is infinitely complex and fraught with danger. Any attempt at providing simple solutions to these complex problems will result only in a compounding of problems. Thus, when the white political prisoner is affronted by "segregated" seating arrangements in prison facilities his first response may be to "desegregate" or, we should say, "re-integrate" those units which black militants have so assiduously made "separate" and, in their eyes, "more than equal." To try to reconstruct a community of racial harmony, brotherhood, and accord which, in truth, never existed even when the facilities were not "segregated" is to employ a solution which does great harm. The invariable result of such oversimplification is the unceremonious—often forcible—rejection of the white intruder.

So-called segregated facilities have a meaning for the black inmate which most white political prisoners cannot be expected fully to appreciate. To impose one's white standard, however exalted its ultimate aim, is—justifiably, we believe—viewed by black inmates as a demonstration of white arrogance and intolerance. Greater sensitivity to the needs and desires of the black prison community might suggest to political prisoners that respect for the wishes of this community and toleration for its expression of solidarity might be a better approach.

In like manner, political prisoners would be well advised to exhibit an understanding and tolerance for most of the other manifestations of in-prison black power. If, as sometimes happens, a black prisoner intentionally steps in front of one in the chow line, the best course of action is to overlook the incident. Any other response might lead either to a permanent estrangement of white political prisoners from the black community or, in rare instances, a physical conflict which, regardless of its outcome, cannot possibly benefit *any* prisoner. If this policy of patience and forbearance is adhered to, and if, despite snide remarks and overtly hostile acts, the white political prisoner can still maintain an affinity for and an empathy with black militancy, it has been our experience that the artificial barriers of distrust and suspicion will eventually, to some extent, begin to crumble.

Even when racial barricades are lowered, most white political prisoners have wisely refrained from attempting to assume leadership in the black community. Any attempt to do this would be worse than futile and would surely result in the re-creation of the original distrust. It must be understood that the political prisoners' relationship to the black militants is likely to remain a distant one. While most political prisoners understand this, some are still tempted to "infiltrate" the black community by inconspicuously offering advice. Political prisoners are sometimes prone to insinuate that black inmates ought to express their discontent more openly and forcefully. It is the black militant who shoulders the brunt of the retribution for such acts; it is, therefore, his right to choose his own tactics.

The basic and undeniable defect in all such efforts to relate to the black community is that the white political prisoner is using this community to wage the political battle which he is unable or unwilling to wage. He is not needed or wanted by the blacks, the "hillbillies," the so-called organized-crime syndicate inmates, or, indeed, by any bloc of prisoners. He cannot act for himself because he has not chiseled out a distinct, granite-hard identity of his own. The longer he flounders about seeking a group through which he can express his militancy, the more closely will he approach amorphousness. The obvious alternative has thus far only rarely been perceived by political prisoners, who have, in a sense, an identity already created for themselves if they are willing to act in concert.

Political prisoners must begin from their *own* base in initiating actions that, hopefully, both black and white inmates will join togther in, providing that the actions are well-conceived and relate to all inmates. But there are times when white political prisoners should clearly follow black leadership in actions that the latter has initiated. At the USDB, as a case in point, black inmates were ready to strike if the demand for a memorial for Martin Luther King was not met; white political prisoners were ready, rightly so, to join the strike. Another and even more dramatic example of this would be in a situation like the recent take-over in the New York City jails. Black and Puerto Rican inmates, who formed the overwhelming majority, carried out that historic event. If acts like that should occur where white political prisoners are incarcerated, they should not hesitate to give their full support.

Having once charted a course of independent political action and prison resistance under the banner of an organized and disciplined body, the individual white political prisoner may very well discover that he is no longer isolated, no longer a passive spectator, no longer merely a surreptitious agent of change hiding in the shadow of the black militant: rather, he is an active resister of the prison system and its personnel. Inasmuch as he will surely confront racist prison officials, the white resister will offer concrete aid, however indirectly, to the black militant. In the process of fighting under their own banner, political prisoners will, no doubt, earn the sympathy and respect of blacks. If targets are correctly selected, as they should be, victories will benefit all prisoners. By their example, political prisoners may galvanize other prisoners, both white and black, to further action. Thus, even though we do not expect an early amelioration of racial hostility among prisoners, we can still envision occasions when these mutually hostile groups may cooperate to fight the common enemy of all prisoners; eventually, perhaps more lasting alliances will be created.

In closing, we must acknowledge the tentative nature of the foregoing analysis since it is based on present conditions which may, at some time in the future, change. For example, were white and black militants outside of prison to find a common basis for joint struggle, it is to be expected that prison racial attitudes would change accordingly.

Chapter 16

HOMOSEXUALITY

Homosexuality in prison is a difficult and sensitive subject to write about, but it must be faced because it is a significant problem. In Viktor Frankel's book *From Death Camp to Existentialism,* the author says that there was very little thought of sexual matters or perversion in the Nazi concentration camps because, for one, the prisoners were starved and that fact outweighed all other considerations. In American prisons, the inmates are not starved for food; sexually, however, they are emaciated. The very privileges that free one from obsession about where the next meal is coming from, or whether there is adequate shelter or clothing give rise to a grossly abnormal preoccupation with sex, since sexual satisfaction is not permitted.

There are two categories of homosexuals in prison: the passive and the aggressive. At times, one person may possess the characteristics of both types.

The passive homosexual is often noted by his effeminate affectations in speech, manner, and dress. He may also be spotted by his "walking with" his "husband." He is called, among other things, "punk, sissy, fag, bitch, homo." He may have indulged in homosexual activity outside of prison, but in a number of cases, the passive homosexual was not gay on the outside, but pressured into homosexual activity after he was imprisoned. In other cases, the homosexual atmosphere of prison serves to actualize what are latent tendencies outside of prison.

The aggressive homosexual plays the "male" role in the homosexual relationship. He is more difficult to spot because the prison society forces the vast majority of inmates to adopt exaggerated masculine affectations and to completely shun anything that smacks of femininity. In the last analysis the aggressive homosexual is known by his talk and his reputation.

Homosexual rendezvous are arranged under a variety of circumstances so as to avoid detection. The "business" is carried off in a shower room, in a corner of a dormitory, in a cell in the honor block, or anywhere else appropriate. The circumstances vary from institution to institution and from time to time. The lack of privacy makes it nearly impossible for homosexual activity to go unnoticed—at least by other inmates; and if inmates know about it, the administration will soon know: informers abound.

Within the prison society, the passive homosexual is treated with extreme derision but at the same time with unconscious deference. He is a target of constant verbal abuse in daily conversations. Often an argument will end in name-calling—and the names hurled will be punk, sissy, or fag. Homosexuality is not discussed twenty-four hours a day but when it is, the passive homosexual is ridiculed and blamed for nearly everything under the sun, and there are many convincing expressions of genuine hate for him. He, along with the rat or snitch, occupies the lowest rungs of the prison social ladder. Relationships that are possible on the outside (in which each party treats the other as equal and both parties have freely contracted the relationship) are hard to come by on the inside. Homosexual arrangements in prison are made almost exclusively on the basis of force (threatened or actual), not on the basis of free choice. The strongest, most aggressive inmates "cop" the available "homos." And unless he has adequate protection, the passive homosexual will be pressured into unwanted sexual relations by various inmates. The facts of life for most imprisoned, passive homosexuals are demeaning stares, ridicule, social ostracism, and constant seduction. However, we do know of instances in which passive homosexuals have been "lucky" in their initial choice of a protective lover in prison. The lover-protector was a strong but sensitive human being who gave as much as he received. Such relationships have sometimes lasted several years.

On the other hand, once the social situation has been stabilized, that is, once the homosexual is recognized and accepted as such, he is dealt with on that basis. He works with and relates to other inmates and staff members as well as his particular personality permits. He lives in less physical danger now that he has one or more protectors. At the risk of indulging in amateur psychologizing, the passive homosexual is often not abused to his face because a great many inmates are thankful to have someone else play a role which they themselves ambivalently admire and dread. Many inmates do not understand and often are quite afraid of the passive and aggressive homosexual tendencies operative within themselves; but if they have to choose, they will identify with the aggressive tendencies. They will do so in order to avoid gross exploitation, which is the usual lot of the passive homosexual. They will frequently juxtapose their own "masculinity" against the femininity of the passive homosexual. In this way, the passive homosexual provides a means by which a poorly constructed masculine image can puff itself up.

An indication of the status of the passive homosexual lies in the attitudes toward sex as expressed by the entire prison population: anyone who is sodomized is automatically considered inferior. The prevailing male attitude of domination over the female in heterosexual relations is more oppressive and intensified in homosexual relations and therefore stands out in bolder relief. Prison love affairs, then, can hardly promote liberation or revolution.

The prison "wife" is held in the same degraded and sub-
servient position as are women outside of prison. But, as
is also true of life outside of prison, the homosexual is afforded some of the same privileges given to women, or at
least is given special favors which are thought of as
privileges. They are objects upon which to bestow gifts
and they are indulged in their occasional feminine fits of
temper. The passive homosexual is often content to play
out the role expected of him. He may, for example,
threaten, when jilted, to cut up the offending party; or, in
a fit of pique, to now "suck every dick in the joint"—
threats which infrequently materialize.

The incidence of homosexual activity in Federal prisons
is hard to determine. It is our opinion that practicing aggressive and passive homosexuals are a minority of the
prison population. Exactly how much of a minority they
are would depend on one's definition of who fits into the
category of "practicing" homosexual. For instance, the fig-
ure would rise if one included those men who engaged in
homosexual activity on only a few occasions during the
period of their confinement: many prisoners opine that "it
is good to clean out your tubes every once in a while."
When we say that practicing homosexuals are a minority
we are excluding those men who only occasionally in-
dulge, and are referring to men for whom homosexuality
occupies as prominent a place in their daily routine as
heterosexual activity would for most men outside of
prison. But if the active homosexuals compose a minority, the problem itself is anything but minor. The homosexual make-up of prison—the all-male society—grievously
haunts the entire prison population. There is nowhere to
hide, no place to escape. Day in and day out, year in and
year out, sometimes noticeable and sometimes not, the
frustration of living without heterosexual warmth and love

seeps into the bones of every individual. Add to this the
punishment from the repression of homosexual desires and
the effect upon the personalities of the inmates can probably never be fully eradicated; it simply must be lived
with.

Beyond the practicing homosexuals, homosexual behavior continues on another level. There are those inmates
who vicariously engage in homosexual activity by talking
about it, there are those who engage in homosexual playing and joking. At one time or another, the vast majority
of inmates takes part in such pastimes. The major function
of homosexual play is to act out in a limited—and supposedly humorous—way what is forbidden, although av-
idly desired. The play is both a defense against and a par-
tial fulfillment of taboo pleasures. Given the circumstances, it is necessary and performs a significant social
function. The jokes are stale and the play is crass, but all
prisoners are destined to witness it and take part in it
many times over. Often a slip of the tongue will be picked
up by a group of inmates and a forced joke made of it; one
or two inmates may blow kisses to one another to the
amusement of onlookers; a feigned embrace and offer to
go to someone's quarters is sometimes play-acted; and
there are a host of other ways in which homosexual play
is carried on.

We might even say that homosexual activity is a
normal response in the prison situation. This is especially
true for men who are imprisoned for more than two or
three years. Homosexuality, unlike abstention or masturbation, does not indicate a complete physical and emotional withdrawal of the prisoner. There is a redeeming
virtue in the human physical contact necessary in homosexuality which the alternatives do not offer. Then, too,
prisoners are hungry for signs, any signs, of affection and

human warmth. In a society where affection is absent, men are prone to settle for even a bogus variety of affection as expressed in the generally exploitable prison homosexual relationship.

However, for many prisoners the possibility that word of their homosexual activity in prison might leak out to their friends on the outside is a sufficient deterrent to homosexual involvement; their social standing would be compromised. Another impediment is that homosexual activity is against prison regulations. Many men do not want to risk being busted on that account. It is embarrassing and harmful to have a bust for homosexuality on one's record in terms of hopes for early parole. Homosexual jealousy plays a large part in keeping down the number of aggressive homosexuals. The desired "object" is always in short supply and more than one stabbing has resulted from an infringement on someone's "arrangement." Bourgeois morality is another stumbling block in the way of all-out homosexual activity. Most prisoners have been imbued with an ingrown cultural aversion to homosexuality: the guilt feelings are too great for most prisoners to overcome.

Before detailing the specific problems which political prisoners might face, we had best set the stage by describing the basic techniques that aggressive homosexuals employ to lure and sometimes force other inmates into homosexual activity. There are three basic techniques with variations on each theme. These techniques are time-tested and are used in a conscious, purposeful way. They may be called the hard sell, the soft sell, and the combination hard-and-soft sell.

The hard sell is a verbal—and perhaps physical—assault with little or no warning. A threat or two precedes any action. Pointing to the intended victim's butt, the aggressor might say, "You better get that penitentiary box together, cause it's me and you." Or he might say something else, to the effect of "fuck or fight," after which the worst part of the hard sell might ensue, that is, the intended victim might be physically assaulted and possibly raped. As with the incidence of homosexuality, it would be hard to quantify the number of rape attempts or even the number of actual rapes. As regards political prisoners, we met two in the course of our prison experience who were raped; we knew several others who avoided rape by a physical show of force—perhaps a small skirmish was involved; and there were many others who narrowly escaped rape attempts by being transferred quickly from inside the penitentiary to the "safer" farm camps. We estimate that one out of four political prisoners has had either to defend himself against a physical assault with homosexual intent or was not far from being physically assaulted before reaching the farm camp. The danger is real enough.

The soft sell is a more congenial approach and has a number of different elements. One of them is that, at some point, the "trick" (i.e., the intended target) is openly asked if he will consent to homosexual activity. But the main thrust of the soft sell is a friendly, helpful attitude that, by certain indications, is distinguishable from disinterested friendliness. The soft-seller will be courteous in his offerings of commissary items and will show great interest in discussing any variety of subjects. But an air of insincerity is easily discernible. For the more naive, it may take longer to realize what the "friend" is after.

More common is the combination hard-and-soft sell. The classic example of this is the protection game. Commissary items and friendly talk are offered first. Then the intended victim is told by his benefactor that he is in danger from a certain group: he will offer protection from this group, if an "arrangement" is made. "Arrangements," the victim is told, are respected by everyone. The choice is the easy alternative or the difficult one, and it is stressed that there are no *other* alternatives. To increase pressure and to create a climate in which the intended victim can be placed in an unfavorable light, lies and unfounded rumors may be employed. The target may be told that it has been heard on the prison wire (i.e., rumor mill) that he is a "homo." Or he might be told that another prisoner has admitted to having had a homosexual affair with him. The aggressive homosexual may even start a rumor of his own. While talking and being seen with the intended victim the aggressor may say to others that he already has an arrangement with the individual in question. If the situation persists and the rumor spreads, the lie gains a credence which is nearly impossible to dislodge. Often, once a lie takes hold, the only hope is to minimize its effect rather than openly attempting to set people straight. Guilt by association is a powerful factor in prison life, especially in homosexual matters. There is an inordinate, unhealthy predisposition among most inmates to believe the worst about their fellow convicts. This is a product of the pressures, frustrations, and intense lack of privacy of prison life.

With these techniques, then, the aggressive homosexuals make their approach. But the danger that aggressive homosexual advances pose, and the corresponding alertness to it varies at different stages of imprisonment and at different institutions. For the new prisoner, the danger of homosexual advances is greatest in the early stages of imprisonment. Special alertness is required from the beginning; the county jail, the Federal detention jail, and the Admission and Orientation section of the penitentiary are places in which possible "tricks" are sized up and gone after. Later, when the new prisoner has successfully established himself at the institution, the danger is considerably reduced, and becomes further reduced as time goes on.

Different institutions pose different problems. An adult penitentiary (i.e., Lewisburg) differs from a youth institution (i.e., Petersburg or El Reno). In the adult penitentiary, the approaches are more sophisticated than at the youth institutions. The experienced adults have developed the combination technique more effectively, whereas at the youth institutions the hard sell prevails. However, there are advantages to this. If the newcomer acts quickly and decisively the danger is over sooner, because the young men at these institutions are less accomplished and less persistent than penitentiary prisoners.

The minimum-security farm camps pose the least threat of all. In the case of a young political prisoner, once he reaches the farm or prison camp where he will find other political prisoners of his own age, the danger is almost nonexistent. Only if a particular individual is extremely naive will any difficulty develop. This does not, of course, imply that the sexually torturing atmosphere behind the wall is not also operative at the farm camps: it most assuredly is. The danger is less but the sexual agony is the same on all levels of imprisonment.

In relating the whole question of prison homosexuality to political prisoners we would like to list and describe various factors that conspire to make many political prisoners potential targets for homosexual advances. We would then like to offer some advice on how to deal with them.

The first factor is that most political prisoners are young. Being young in prison is of itself tantamount to being sexually attractive. A concomitant of the attractiveness of youth is the aura of inexperience that is associated with youth. The inexperience of political prisoners with prison life seems more noticeable than is the inexperience of young prisoners convicted of other crimes. The latter are more likely to be wise in the ways of the street and are more likely to put up a defense of violent self-assertiveness. Political prisoners, in comparison, tend to be gentle, and do not project a super-masculine image of toughness. To be both young and gentle is to be in danger.

A second factor is the candor that these prisoners tend to exhibit. Political prisoners are polite, intelligent, articulate, and usually pleased to explain their position and actions to anyone who will listen, or to anyone who questions them. Politics and religion are their business. These brought them to prison and because of that it is felt that an explanation is due. Bank-robbing needs no similar defense; it is self-explanatory. But in prison there is a danger in being too candid. New inmates are sized up by established prisoners very quickly. First impressions are lasting, and an initial blunder may be costly in terms of the problems it may engender, conceivably, for the duration of one's confinement. Being too open and talkative is usually considered a come-on by aggressive homosexuals.

A third factor is the independence generally exhibited by most political prisoners. The independence we speak of is a tendency, almost a practice, not to identify strongly or quickly with a particular clique. Hillbillies hang out with one another, narcotics pushers talk to each other about the business of selling dope, inmates who were involved in so-called organized crime associate with one another, block "homies" (men from the same city or town), those from Washington or New York stick together, etc. The political prisoner, on the other hand, tends to be, though affable, more of a loner. But there is a danger in being a loner because a loner sticks out; in more practical terms, the loner finds it more difficult to protect himself.

A fourth factor specifically concerns the manner by which white political prisoners relate to the black-liberation struggle. White political prisoners tend to be sympathetic to that struggle and on occasion, a black aggressive homosexual can use the white political prisoner's sympathy as an inroad to a homosexual relationship. This is especially likely to occur when naïveté outstrips clear thinking. The point must be starkly presented: it is dangerous in the first stages of imprisonment for a young white prisoner to associate freely with black inmates. If a young white prisoner is seen fraternizing extensively with black inmates, and especially if he is seen talking with well-known black homosexuals, the majority of white inmates is preconditioned to believe the worst. As a matter of fact, some black inmates will themselves interpret what may essentially be an inexperienced liberal attitude as being an overture for protection. If one flaunts his pretentious liberal attitudes, and eats and talks with black inmates, he will only get himself in trouble; in fact, black inmates couldn't care less about eating with him. The response will most likely be the same as that received by one political prisoner in the penitentiary: he was approached by a brother who said, "I hear you're a nigger lover, prove it." This response is less of a reflection on the brother and more of a reflection on the inexperience and poor judgment of the white inmate.

The fifth factor is the inability or reluctance of many political prisoners to act decisively and forcefully in the face of homosexual advances. There may be many reasons for this outlook but it must be realized that to vacillate or to appear hesitant only serves as an invitation.

It is clear that a young prisoner cannot alter his age, but he *can* be more self-conscious about his person. For example, a young prisoner simply cannot afford to allow himself to project any characteristic that might be considered effeminate: this includes forms of posture, speech, and grooming. Experienced prisoners have an uncanny ability to size up new prisoners. Because of the perverted situation in which many inmates affect an exaggerated masculinity, effeminacy stands out immediately. The novice must realize that what is not noticed on the outside, such as long hair, may be seized upon as an indication of homosexuality in prison.

In the case of a passive homosexual who clearly flaunts effeminate characteristics, he is immediately spotted. If such an individual swishes into the county jail or the A&O section of the penitentiary, the chances are very high indeed that he will be approached and taken to bed by one, and often by more than one, inmate before his first night is over. Word of the "new homo" spreads like wildfire and the effeminate passive homosexual has little chance against the odds he faces. It seems that resignation is the usual course taken by these individuals, with the hope that a better arrangement can be worked out later on.

The young prisoner, who in lieu of a shortage of passive homosexuals might face advances himself, is well advised to acquire a good degree of modesty about his body. He should dress and undress quickly, and not hang around the shower room, but shower with dispatch, preferably when the shower room is least crowded. If he does not mind his ass, somebody else will.

It sometimes happens in the penitentiary that political prisoners get themselves into a jam. By making any one of the mistakes touched upon, they find themselves in situations that they have to get out of fast. Such situations develop most frequently in the A&O section of the penitentiary and in the "jungle" dormitories where some political prisoners spend a few weeks before going to the farm camp. At such times one of the most commonly employed means of extricating oneself from a possible jam is by checking into the segregation unit. This can be done in a number of ways: one can refuse to report to work, one can tell the lieutenant that he is being bothered and wants out, one can have a friend tell the lieutenant for him. *Under no circumstances* do we advise anyone to point out to prison officials those specific individuals who might be making threats, nor do we advise that anyone threaten an inmate with such a report. But if a situation seems to have gotten out of hand, and if the prisoner thinks that he can't handle it, then he should feel no shame and make no hesitation in checking into segregation. However, our hope is that future political prisoners will be wise enough *not* to get themselves into jams. Also, if the first time an advance is made, one acts as if he is ready to "bust some motherfuckin' ass," that is, in our opinion, better than having to check into segregation.

The candor that most political prisoners exhibit must be significantly curtailed. We do not suggest that one make a practice of insulting people, but we do say that one must be wary, uncommunicative, and sometimes rude with a majority of inmates. As the political inmate becomes jail-wise, he can alter this approach, but in the beginning it is necessary. It may seem strange at first but one must discipline oneself so as to ignore a large number of people with whom one is in close physical proximity. We mean that it is sometimes necessary to avert one's eyes from direct eye contact with other inmates, and avoid visual as well as verbal communication. *Friendly attitudes just will not do.*

Group solidarity must be substituted for independence. At almost every Federal institution, there are several political prisoners. The novice and the established political prisoner must seek one another out. They should dine together, spend leisure time together, and rap together. The established political prisoner must awaken the novice to the major aspects of life in the institution. Among other things, the novice must have pointed out, for his benefit, those inmates with whom it might be dangerous to associate. If there are no political prisoners around, the novice should find the next safest groups of inmates to associate with. These would be the white-collar criminals, potheads, acid heads, and select JW's. However, trying to categorize "safe" groups is risky. Decisions must be made individually, and with one's eyes open.

In avoiding possible homosexual advances, there are two groups of inmates one should take special pains to sidestep. They are the notorious aggressive homosexuals and the obvious passive homosexuals. We have tried to make it clear why one should avoid the former, but there are also good reasons to avoid the latter as well. Most political prisoners do not feel compelled to hate passive homosexuals. On the contrary, liberal, humanitarian, civil-libertarian views tend to make political prisoners sympathetic to their plight, and often lead to attempts to befriend them: this is risky on two counts. One might be accused of trying to mess with someone else's "woman"; or, one may be placed in the same category by virtue of guilt by association. We were acquainted with one political prisoner who had his face slapped by an aggressive homosexual simply because he had quite innocently said "hello" while passing the homosexual's "woman" in the hallway. He was accused of having tried to get a "piece of the action."

Finally, there is an aspect of the homosexual scene called "blocking." Blocking means that a third party deliberately moves between a homosexual advancer and his object. This is done by rapping, eating, and taking recreation with the intended trick, while the advancer is trying to do the same in the hope of making a score. Blocking is a dangerous pastime, especially in the penitentiary. Someone blocking a potential score may find himself in a worse jam than the score is in. But the authors' experience has shown that a limited form of blocking is necessary if experienced political prisoners are to protect some of the more naive new ones. Even at the farm camps blocking may be required, especially if word gets around that a newly arrived young man had "trouble" inside the penitentiary. When it may become necessary to do some blocking, it has to be done with caution and in a very cool manner: one must take pains to act as if he is not aware of what he is doing.

If the above cautions are heeded, it is hoped that homosexual advances can be avoided altogether; that is best, by far. But if such advances do occur, it is important to meet them forcefully and decisively. Curt, even hostile, remarks are in order. "No, man. You must be crazy." "Get out of my face." "You can try whatever you want if you want your head busted." If possible, one may be able to turn the situation around by making a joke; a joke helps the other guy save face. That is, it doesn't put him in the position, necessarily, of having to respond to a counter-threat or else back down. At the same time, a good joke gives the impression that one is not as naive as he looks and that he would fight if pressed. One might smile and say, "Sure, man, you can have all the ass you want after I stick my dick in *your* cakes. Tit for tat, right?"

Our experience has shown us that verbal and physical force, in response to aggressive homosexual advances, has almost always ended successfully for the intended victim. The aggressor was not beaten; he was repulsed and went away. He may have said, "This isn't the end. I'll get you later." But if he and his friends were subsequently studiously avoided by the intended victim, the latter would usually be left alone after that. A grudge or bad feelings may have been held for a time, but in due time even they dissipate. One does not have to be a killer to ward off these advances. A show of force is usually sufficient. If extreme trouble occurs, we recommend that the individual defend himself physically, but we wish to emphasize that a physical defense is a last resort. Inmates should, whenever possible, avoid fighting with one another. Inmate fights mainly benefit the prison authorities, and weaken the likelihood that inmate solidarity against their common oppressor will develop.

This brings us to our final consideration, the role of the administration in prison homosexuality. The prison officials' role is crucial and determinant since it is they who possess the power.

Officially, consenting homosexual relations are forbidden by prison regulations. At the USDB, even masturbation is forbidden. Needless to say, forced homosexual relations are also forbidden and may be punished by law. But the official position of the administration, and their protestations to the effect that they are combating the problem, do not correspond with their real practices and desires.

The more notorious passive homosexuals are usually quartered in a specific cell block, where supposedly they can be watched more closely. Periodically, consenting homosexuals may be busted if they are too indiscreet, or if a tightening of the strings is deemed necessary. They might lose some good time and perhaps, temporarily, some other privileges. In the case of homosexual rape, it is the practice of the prison administration to admit as little as possible. If they can, they will try to discredit the reputation of the *victim*. They may allege that he was always a passive homosexual and invited the attack. If the administrators cannot do that, they will do everything they can to see to it that "rape" cases are never brought into Federal court, where the lights burn too brightly.

Often, the prison authorities will admit that homosexuality exists in prison but that it is hard to deal with and eradicate; they say that it is difficult to detect and hence, control. When asked specifically about the problems of young prisoners, they say that they have no idea who may or who may not have problems. We do not buy the administration line. Our experience has brought us to the conclusion that the administrators profit by the perverted and poisonous atmosphere which they themselves maintain. We further believe that they consciously use the exploitable homosexual atmosphere to further their own ends.

To begin with, the prison administration is thoroughly committed to punishment by sexual deprivation. It is the single most important component of our punitive and vindictive prison system. Secondly, the administration allows the homosexual vigilante aura to exist because it acts as a threat to inmates. Specifically, the jungle dormitories of every penitentiary are used by officials to threaten and intimidate prisoners with homosexual rape. When the prison officials place a young prisoner, political or not, in the jungle, they are saying in effect, "Go ahead men, see what you can do with him." It may not serve the administration's purpose to have a young prisoner actually assaulted but the *threat* of rape does serve its purpose. It induces all inmates, especially the younger, less apathetic ones, to cooperate, to get out of the jungle and stay out. The message is, "Keep in line, boy, or lose your ass." Finally, preoccupation with their sexual frustration acts to divert the prisoners from confronting the enemy—the prison administration. It also plays havoc with inmate solidarity, because some inmates are forced to prey upon other inmates. As a result, all inmates must be on guard against being taken advantage of.

One final fact that liberals, radicals, and revolutionaries must appreciate is that a simple exposé of the problem—including proof of homosexual rape attempts—is not enough. The administration is ruthless. In order to appease and mollify public opinion, it will punish unmercifully the alleged homosexual attackers who are themselves victims and who have been severely punished in the first place by the penal system. The exposé approach, in the absence of concomitant legal and political pressure, simply results in punishment for *all* the victims. The enemy—the prison Establishment—is left virtually unconfronted.

There is a position with which the authors are familiar and that should be raised in this chapter. It concerns those political activists who are homosexuals and who, finding themselves in prison, think they should take an open stand on the issue while there. These men say that fulfilling sexual desires greatly increases one's ability to deal with the dehumanizing life of prison; they say that an open stand on homosexuality is a better political position than hiding it.

However, homosexual activity in prison is contrary to regulations. If inmates are caught in such activity, or if they are ratted upon by other inmates, the "culprits" can lose good time and a reasonable chance for parole. They can be put in segregation, conceivably for long periods of time, if they are constant offenders. Redress to the courts for these rights does not seem to help. Recently, six men at Atlanta Federal Penitentiary drew up a writ asking that they be permitted to write to their "husbands" on the outside. The Federal judge in that district wrote a blistering reply, saying that he was not going to be a party to "perversion," and denied the writ. (One of the complainants later remarked that he didn't recall inviting the judge to his party.) It is clear, therefore, that even if an individual admits and defends his homosexuality among inmates and staff, actual participation must be pursued in secret—or one must be prepared for further punishment. A very important consideration that must be taken into account is that known homosexuals, i.e., those who have been caught, are not given the opportunity of residing at the farm camps: they are kept behind the walls of the penitentiary or the correctional institute. If inmates at a farm camp are caught in homosexual activity, they are busted back to the wall.

We have indicated that passive homosexuals are held in derision by the vast majority of inmates. As a rule, they find themselves the prey of tough, sexually deprived inmates. But we want to make clear that passive homosexuals do not necessarily face constant, unwanted, and adverse attention: some are constant prey but others are not. Two inmates come to mind: the first a slight, thin brother in his early thirties who bore exaggerated feminine affectations—he was a freewheeling "homo" who played the field. But it was clear from all accounts that this inmate called his own shots. He was a tough-minded but exuberant person with a strong personality. A comment by another inmate that stuck in our minds was, "You better believe that _____ can take care of 'herself.'" About the second, we heard the following story. A big, muscular inmate approached him and intimidated him into performing homosexual relations. At a not much later date the offended individual went up to his attacker while the latter slept and with three razor blades between the fingers of a clenched fist ran them down the man's face. No one bothers that passive homosexual anymore. This may be just a "prison story" but the spirit of it is true. Along with the description of the man we know, it brings home our point. It *is* possible for a passive homosexual in prison to avoid exploitation; but it is a hard row to hoe. Both of the men above can defend themselves, but they seem to be exceptions. Most of the homosexuals we know both in and out of prison are not determined enough to be able to "control their own bodies" in a prison setting.

However, if homosexual militancy continues to grow, then the political activist, who may also be a militant homosexual, may be sufficiently prepared to deal openly with the issue of homosexuality if he finds himself in prison. Militant homosexuality, prepared verbally and physically to defend itself, is a good and important development. If it can be done successfully in prison, we think that it is better—psychologically *and* politically—for all concerned that homosexuality be placed out in the open and defended.

(The following addendum is by David Miller.)

When I came through Lewisburg the first time, I was in a low frame of mind. The walled penitentiary was imposing. In A&O I was apprehensive when night came. I heard inmates talking about "taking people off," and stayed awake in my bunk until 3:00 or 4:00 A.M. What actually happened that night was that eight or ten inmates took turns in bed with a tall, thin brother who had arrived that day. I don't know whether the brother encouraged them or was pressured into it; he possessed many of the "feminine" affectations of speech and posture that make such an individual an immediate target of aggressive homosexuals. I was shipped out to Allenwood in a few days. There was not much danger of physical homosexual attack there and my fears receded quickly. It wasn't until seven months later, when I was transferred back to the penitentiary, that I ran into trouble. One might have expected that in seven months, even at Allenwood, I would have gained enough insight not to fall into any traps. Unfortunately, that was not so.

Back at the penitentiary I was quartered in a dreary basement dormitory called K-1. We had to look up to see the sidewalk outside. It wasn't quite a "jungle" dormitory but it wasn't far from it. I was put to work in the kitchen, first in the dish room, then wiping tables and mopping. I had decided to work and to live in "population" instead of refusing work and going into segregation, even though there were a dozen political prisoners already there. I knew I wouldn't be put in with them even if I refused work, and I wanted to avoid, if possible, a transfer out of the area, to Sandstone, Minnesota, for instance. I was in the population at Lewisburg for a month; trouble developed during that time because of my naïveté and also because I was a victim of circumstances. I made several mistakes and I had mistakes made for me.

I tended to stay alone a lot and didn't bother to seek out one or two "rap partners" to hang around with. I was too friendly with black inmates, even though I didn't hang out with any in particular. (I got to know black inmates right away because I started playing both intramural and all-star basketball, and the vast majority of the basketball players were black.) Often I would get on the black line in the dining hall. I was also too friendly with the black passive homosexual working in the same section of the

dining hall as I; and he was the most sought after passive homosexual in the joint. But the associations that
were the source of the most trouble were with two young,
white, Selective-Service violators. One was an introverted
quiet guy from the D.C. area, at Lewisburg for a ninety-
day psychiatric-observation period before going back to
court for sentencing. The psychiatric-observation cases
are kept behind the wall, and are usually quartered in one
of the jungle dormitories; it was a bad place for this young
man to be. The second Selective-Service violator was also
from the D.C. area. He was in A&O and I saw him in the
dining hall and at yard time. Both of these men were harassed, often by aggressive homosexuals, almost from the
day they each came to the penitentiary. To associate with
them conspired to make me into a target.

A brother who was moving in on the quiet guy (although I didn't know it at the time), approached me and
asked me if I knew him. I said I did. He said that a lot of
guys were talking about him and that it would be a good
idea if I hung out with him more—as a kind of protection
for him. I said that I would, not appreciating that it was
part of a setup. A partner of this brother also approached
me and said the same thing. He added that some guys
had expressed interest in me, too, and did I know how to
handle that. I said yes, *still* not appreciating what was going on, nor how to handle it. At another point, the latter
asked if I would meet him at the movies. I didn't; the
movies are a notorious homosexual rendezvous.

I found myself, a day or two later, having a talk with
these two brothers. Their game was as follows: I was putting them in a bad spot; they said that they were being
pressured from some guys who wanted to take me off; but
those guys would lay off if these two and I let it be known
that we had an "arrangement." They put in a few scare

stories about being ripped off, like how bad it was at Marion (the penitentiary). They made up an idiotic story about how some guys thought I was a snitch because I was sent back to the penitentiary and then, right after that, twelve political prisoners were sent back too. I told them that I wasn't interested in an arrangement. I started to tell them something about myself and to ask them about themselves but soon realized that it was ridiculous. I finally said there was no arrangement and that I would think of a way to avoid any rip off. They didn't think I could avoid it, and we parted on that "cordial" note.

I didn't sleep well that night. I had gotten myself into a jam. I wasn't sure about fighting if it came to that; I still did not think in terms of violent self-defense. Anyway, it seemed that the odds were against me—the lies that these guys were spreading seemed to have taken hold. I decided to avoid the trouble by going to segregation, so in the morning I refused to go to work in the kitchen. Instead, I sat down in front of the gate at the control center that leads to the associate warden's offices, and sang a freedom song. (I didn't have to go through the sit-in thing to get locked up but I did it anyway.) In five minutes I was carried to the hole by several hacks. One called me a lot of names to try to get me to react so that the others would have an excuse to beat me. I didn't react and was sent up to the segregation unit on the third floor.

Meanwhile, the second young draft-resister had already gone to segregation and subsequently had been shipped out to Allenwood: he had been even more naive than I. Guys in A&O would offer him a full pack of cigarettes after he had tried to bum only one—and he would take the pack. One guy tried to force him to the floor in the john but he held his ground successfully, without hitting back, and the guy gave up. He told me at dinner that he was going to be moved that afternoon from A&O to E-1, a jungle dorm. I told him that that wasn't a bright prospect, and he said that somebody had to confront the situation. Fortunately, a friend of his told the lieutenant on duty that this young man was having trouble. After the 10:00 P.M. count, a hack went to E-1 and fetched him. After being in segregation for a day, he was sent to Allenwood.

The other Selective-Service violator did not fare as well. A week or so after I went to segregation I heard that the quiet guy had been forced into relations with a group of ten inmates, and was now in the hospital. I was saddened and angry. Evidently, he had not seen the situation building up as it had. He didn't take the necessary step of getting out of it by going to segregation; maybe he hadn't realized or had refused to admit to himself the seriousness of the situation. Later, when he went back to court for sentencing, this incident and the report of the psychiatrist saved him from a prison sentence: he was given probation. But it was a hard way to get out of prison.

I stayed in segregation for a month. Locked in a cell twenty-four hours a day except for a shower once a week and for visits from my wife, I read (a few books floated around the segregation unit) and sang country songs with a couple of guys in cells near mine. I intended to stay there for two months, then ask to be sent to the farm outside the wall or transferred to another joint. I knew they wouldn't send me back to Allenwood; certainly, it was highly unlikely. But before I requested anything, an associate warden called me to his office and said that he had gotten a call from a friend of mine on the outside asking if I had "trouble" with other prisoners at Lewisburg. (I was annoyed because I didn't ask anyone to do that for me; the person did it on his own, probably after talking with my wife.) I didn't admit to anything in front of the associate warden, but I did say that I was willing to work if I were sent to the farm camp, and that I preferred not to be put back in population. Which, translated, meant that I would sooner be transferred anywhere than live and work in the population at that time. The AW was not stupid and knew the reason I didn't want to return to population, even though I didn't admit it. He asked if I had heard about the young man who had been physically assaulted. I said yes. He said it was terrible and I agreed. Then he tried to get me to agree that the men who did it were "animals." Two days later, after more than a month in segregation, I was moved to the farm camp.

When I arrived, I immediately sought out Howard Levy and Donald Baty. I knew that they were there since I had met them when they came "through the wall." I caught up with them at suppertime. That evening I ran the whole thing down to them, and from then on hung out nearly exclusively with Howard and Don, except of course during working hours. I carved out my niche with the two white political prisoners at the camp, and avoided almost every other inmate or cut conversations short if begun. It was necessary for me to do this at that time, since I had to regain my standing. I was aware that some dudes were talking behind my back, but because I was uncommunicative and hung out only with Howard and Don, the talk faded. It took less than a month for this unfavorable attention to be neutralized. After that, I found my place, and I could be more relaxed and move more freely among the inmates. What Howard and Don offered was group status —which is more powerful than a lone man, no matter how much of a killer he may be. I gained that status in a short time. But I was aware that I had had to work for it and could not make any more mistakes.

Soon I had acquired all of the affectations and attitudes

necessary. I knew how to be cool and curt, and how to side-step those inmates who were dangerous—especially inside the wall; I knew how to give and take and roll with the jokes about who was going to suck whose dick and who was going to put his foot up whose ass; I knew which inmates *not* to joke with. I went back inside the wall many times, mainly to play intramural and all-star basketball, but also for visits and to attend college-seminar classes. I didn't go back inside on a regular basis until several months after going to the farm camp, when the basketball season rolled around. I noticed some talk at first but it disappeared quickly because I "carried" myself much differently than before. The combination of in-group status, carrying myself better, being a good dude and minding my business, and being a "smoker" on the court proved to eliminate any further trouble.

It is clear that there are differing kinds of help and advice that certain political prisoners need. The two young men inside the wall at Lewisburg could have been given no advice other than to check into segregation and go to the farm camp: it would not have worked for one or two political prisoners inside the wall to hang around with these men to protect them from unwanted advances—that would have jeopardized everyone. The two inmates in question were too naive at the time to help themselves, and they couldn't adapt fast enough to be able to deal successfully with penitentiary life: they simply had to get out. Other political prisoners might be heading for trouble but a few words of advice and redirection on whom to associate with would usually be sufficient in order for them to side-step potential difficulties. This was the case with me after I learned what was up.

Later, the roles changed. I was a member of the in group, and another political prisoner and I took each new political prisoner that came to the camp under our wing. There was one young man who came out to the camp several weeks before I was released; he had had trouble in the wall, and it was well known. A brother at the camp, a very gregarious person, came up to me and suggested that I take this new guy under my wing, that he was really a good kid; I was doing it anyway. Whenever I heard that a new political prisoner had arrived inside the wall, I did my best to get inside and see him as soon as possible. For as long as we had to talk—whether in the yard or at lunch—I hipped him to the prison scene, including advice on homosexual advances. Most of them would say "Yeah, yeah"—but I didn't think that it had sunk in. I found it difficult to communicate the necessary survival techniques to guys who had not been well prepared enough before coming to prison. I knew that they would be hardened by the end of their bits, but I wanted to help them avoid a long, stormy road. A few times, however, I received word that so and so had checked into segregation and was shipped to Allenwood the next day. Certainly, the hipping and hardening process should start before prison.

Chapter 17   RESISTANCE

Prison resistance might conceivably encompass all of the myriad levels of psychic and overt resistance to imprisonment on the part of the imprisoned. For our purposes, however, it is necessary to narrow the focus. On the psychic level, one may hear an inmate say that he is resisting in his own "special way," and that the authorities are not really getting to him. One will hear chronic bitching on the part of inmates, and witness instances of petty thievery at the expense of guards and officials, the smuggling of contraband items, minor acts of sabotage and the like. We do not say that this kind of resistance is of no importance in the life of the institution: the fact is that the majority of inmates, political prisoners included, take part in such activity at one time or another. However, this form of resistance properly belongs to what Erving Goffman, in *Asylums,* calls the "underlife" of the institution. It is a way of "making it" in a prison environment and a defense of personal integrity. It is not, essentially, a threat to the authorities. Even physical violence—short of full-scale rioting—is not a substantial threat to the prison system. In the greatest number of cases, it has no political import because of a lack of organization and articulated demands.

Organized prison resistance is something else again. In organized resistance, basic demands constitute basic *challenges* to the system. There are three general approaches by which such resistance may manifest itself: the legal, the administrative, and the confrontation—although they are not mutually exclusive. They are certainly not even the possession of political prisoners alone. On the contrary, organized resistance has a history as long as imprisonment, with many nonpolitical prisoners leading the way. However, since this book largely deals with political prisoners, our analysis will be limited to their resistance efforts.

In some prison situations, confrontation-oriented resistance, while always a possibility, may (realistically) be deemed inadvisable. When, for example, a political prisoner finds himself isolated from other political prisoners, or finds that he is unable to communicate with the outside world, overt resistance becomes both more difficult and more risky. In military prisons, the threat of a court-martial on a spurious charge of mutiny drastically escalates the risk: one may, therefore, seek an alternative approach. In such circumstances, an administrative or legal attack may be most appealing. Not to be overlooked is the fact that there are times and situations when a legal or administrative form of resistance is simply the best choice, since it may be the most suitable for the occasion.

The legal approach rests upon the presumption that many prison regulations are palpably illegal and unconstitutional. The administrative approach, on the other hand, presumes that prison officials frequently violate their own rules and regulations, and that these violations may be used as a point of leverage in dealing with these same officials. In practice, the legal and administrative approaches are not separate and distinct categories; each complements the other.

Prisoners have, for some time, been permitted to write briefs on their own behalf. Recently, the Supreme Court has also affirmed the right of the prison writ-writer—a "jailhouse lawyer"—to serve the legal needs of other inmates. This decision potentially opens up new vistas for political prisoners challenging the prerogatives of prison administrators.

The prospective political prisoner should be particularly knowledgeable about the legal scope and ramifications of the First, Fifth, and Sixth Amendment rights. The political prisoner should also, upon entering prison, make inquiries concerning the written rules of the institution in which he will be confined and he should request, as well, the written directives published by the Federal Bureau of Prisons concerning *all* Federal prisons. These rules and directives should, in theory, be available upon request, but it may be anticipated that the authorities will be reluctant to divulge this information: hence, the political prisoner's attorney may have to be prevailed upon to obtain this material. A request from a lawyer for these written materials can hardly be denied, but if no lawyer is available to the prospective prisoner he can file his own writ in Federal court demanding access to these documents. As soon as the prospective prisoner—or his lawyer—requests to see and read these public documents he has, in effect, begun to resist, since the mere filing of such a request invariably makes prison officials "uptight" and defensive. Once the documents have been obtained and studied, the prospective prisoner, after incarceration, will be in a better position to assess how well or poorly prison officials heed their own rules and regulations. When they step out of line and violate the rules, he is then in a position to challenge their misuse of authority.

A few examples: in some prisons, liberal and radical magazines, newspapers, and newsletters are, as we have pointed out, censored and banned. This would seem, at face value, to be an infringement of every prisoner's First Amendment rights and should be subject to remedy by the courts, despite their reluctance, until now, to involve themselves in what they regard as the "administrative" decisions of prison officials. But before a test case can ever reach the courts, the prisoner must first initiate several simple, preparatory steps. He must first "set up the case" by requesting, in writing, permission from prison officials to receive the periodicals in question. Duplicate copies of all such written requests must be maintained. Since the final objective is to win the court case and not simply to embarrass prison officials by exposing their illiberal attitudes, it is best to select the least inflammatory periodicals from the list of publications which prison officials find objectionable. It would not be advisable to select for a test case a magazine which features nudity, since prison officials can present "expert" witnesses who may testify that such material is deleterious to the morale of inmates. *The point is not whether or not prison officials are correct.* What the resister is attempting to do is to give prison officials no alternative but to face his issues on his terms. When, as usually happens, the initial request is denied, the next step is to "appeal" the original decision, through the proper channels, to the highest man on the prison totem pole. If, at that point, the institution still denies the request, it is time to notify one's lawyer or to prepare to file a writ demanding relief from the courts.

The combination of legal and administrative confrontation we have just outlined can have only one of two results: either the prison officials accede to the demands, or the case is taken to court—at which point the resultant publicity may embarrass the prison and the government. The point is, that because of the manner in which the case was originally set up, the resister must, irrespective of the court's final decision, win. If the court's verdict is favorable, the next step is for the prisoner to go back to the proscribed list of publications and begin again—this time, with the more "inflammatory" periodicals. Obviously, this approach need not be confined to censorship issues and can be used, with modifications, to suit any number of prison rules and regulations.

The technique is very simple and infinitely adaptable. Its efficiency depends upon the fact that prison officials have, in the past, been so infrequently and weakly challenged that they have developed a sense of omnipotence. Hence, any challenge to their authority is viewed with great alarm, and they can be counted upon to react so inappropriately that they themselves will aggravate the situation.

We find ourselves at a loss to generalize about the ways in which political prisoners are currently employing direct-action confrontation tactics. These vary from institution to institution and thus far no overall strategy has clearly emerged from the struggle. The struggle is being pursued with varying intensity, and to give some flavor of it we will present specific examples of political resistance at three very different institutions: the United States Disciplinary Barracks, the Allenwood Prison Farm Camp, and the Petersburg Federal Reformatory.

UNITED STATES DISCIPLINARY BARRACKS

At the USDB, prison resistance cannot be separated from the political prisoners' attitude to that prison's officials. This attitude can only be described as one of contempt and derision, although the form which our contempt assumed varied from inmate to inmate. Some political prisoners merely ignored the presence and, indeed, the existence of officials, who were viewed as anonymous beings. These inmates simply avoided contact with them, and when a meeting was inevitable they replied curtly—or not at all—to their inquiries.

Other political prisoners were not averse to speaking

with officials, but did so in a derogatory and mocking way, preferably before an audience of inmates. Both methods led to the same result: we demonstrated for our "superior" officers a disrespect which at times bordered on insubordination. In talking with officials it was never our intent to provide them with an understanding of the plight of prisoners; nor did we feel that it was possible to achieve, through reasonable discourse, more compassionate treatment of prisoners. We had long before learned the absolute impossibility of meaningful dialogue with military officials. Rather, some of us spoke with them because we felt that by doing so we could more easily discredit and delegitimize these officials before our fellow prisoners.

Our unbending, absolutist attitude was predicated upon two major premises: first, USDB officials were our adversaries and we could see no moral, political, or utilitarian excuse for a softer attitude; second, many prisoners had not received a discharge from the military and, in a matter of just a few months, would be returned to duty. It was our hope that our resistance to the illegitimate authority of "superiors" might influence those returning to emulate our example, and thus contribute to the worsening morale throughout the armed forces. How well or badly we succeeded it is impossible to gauge, but it is certain that our spirit of struggle was of inestimable value in maintaining our *own* morale at a high level; beyond that, we did certainly win the respect of our fellow prisoners.

One specific example might throw some light upon the possible efficacy of this amorphous but perfectly self-conscious approach. At the USDB, army officials had instituted a retraining program for AWOL offenders who, it was hoped, could be "rehabilitated to return to military duty." For several weeks, the inmates attended military-indoctrination sessions and were put through a modified basic-training program. This program had been in existence at the institution for about a year and had become the pride and joy of USDB officials, since a high percentage of retrainees ultimately completed their tours of duty successfully. It is worthy of note that this program had been devised and designed by the prison's Mental Health Clinic.

With the implementation of our attitudinal approach, together with a counter-political-educational process informally taught by political prisoners, the retraining program gradually deteriorated. More and more men learned how to resist the indoctrination, and before long the entire program was undermined. It has since been discontinued at the USDB, and been transferred to Fort Riley, Kansas, where, it was hoped, it would be more successful since, presumably, it would not be contaminated by political prisoners' irreverence toward military authority and discipline. Following this relocation, several rebellions in protest against the retraining cycle have taken place at Fort Riley.

There were occasions at the USDB when more overt tactics were employed; more often than not, they took the form of administrative resistance. For example, political prisoners decided that they could profit from the availability of Unitarian-Universalist church services. After it had been determined that we could expect the cooperation of the Unitarian-Universalist church in Boston, some fifty written requests were filed with prison officials, demanding that these services be provided. As expected, the officials reacted hostilely to our demands; but continued pressure, together with the threat of ACLU intervention on behalf of political prisoners, forced them to capitulate to our demands. This was a good example of providing "no-win" options for prison authorities. Outside religious services were already being provided by other religious denominations, and to allow a freedom-of-religion case to go to court would have been, from the army's point of view, nonsensical. Foreseeing the potentially explosive publicity attendant upon a court challenge, USDB officials were reluctantly compelled to approve our Unitarian-Universalist services even though they knew, as well as we did, that the services and discussion sessions would center around opposition to the Vietnam war, conscription, and militarism. From the point of view of political prisoners at the USDB, either alternative chosen by the institution was satisfactory: we definitely desired the religious services; on the other hand, we were not at all averse to a legal confrontation, if that had become necessary.

All of us felt that to be effective we had to maintain a position of maximum flexibility. Thus, although there were no specific instances of the use of a confrontation approach, we were well aware that this technique was of potential value—even if only held in reserve. When Martin Luther King was assassinated, black prisoners, led by black political prisoners Ron Lockman and James Johnson, initiated requests for memorial services for the slain civil-rights leader. These requests were initially denied by the officials, but when black prisoners made it known that a work stoppage would ensue if the requests were not granted, they quickly back-tracked and the services were held. It may be noted in passing that white political prisoners played only a subsidiary role in that particular struggle; however, it is most likely that had a work stoppage been called, they would have joined with their black brothers in a general strike.

Another black-led protest involved a demand for the initiation of a course in Afro-American history within the education department. That campaign was handled largely by Roger Harris, a black prisoner. Harris, while propa-

gandizing effectively for the support of other black inmates, was also preparing to appeal to black civil-rights
advocates as well as black congressmen. Prison officials
eventually capitulated to his demands, since they were
fearful that Harris could, with no difficulty, have substan-
tiated his allegations of racism on the part of USDB officials (*see* "Race Relations"). Unfortunately, following
Harris's release from prison, the authorities quietly discontinued the Afro-American history course.

Prison officials are adept at the duplicitous technique of
temporarily acceding to prisoners' demands, only to undo
the newly instituted reforms after the prisoner instigators
of those reforms are removed or released from the prison.
We were acutely aware of this at the USDB, and strove to
redevelop—with each new group of incoming prisoners—
new leadership cadres. Therefore, much of our resistance
took the form of informal lectures, rap sessions, and discussion groups. Our classroom might be anywhere that
men congregated—the chapel, recreation field, hobby shop,
library, etc. In addition to using the mistakes of our official
tormentors as laboratory teaching devices, we also discussed a wide range of politico-economic subjects, since
we were interested in ultimately encouraging as many
prisoners as possible to join, following release, the political struggles which were then rampant in civilian society
and the military.

—HOWARD LEVY

ALLENWOOD PRISON FARM CAMP

The first event occurred on December 21, 1968, when
many people gathered at Allenwood under the sponsorship

of the Quaker Action Committee of Philadelphia. They
came for a day, to visit "prisoners of conscience." The affair was arranged through the Bureau of Prison's chief in
Washington, Myrl Alexander. Although several thousand
people arrived at the farm camp only seven or eight hundred ever got to visit with the political prisoners. Later
that night and the next day, most of the thousands attended a rally and participated in workshops held on the
Bucknell University campus, near the prison. There was
actually no "resistance"·on those days and the details of
the visit are not as important as what preceded it. In terms
of prison resistance, the important achievement lay in the
fact that the visit forced the political prisoners at Allenwood to come together as a group, and discuss our response to the coming events of the twenty-first. We certainly could not avoid dealing with the visit, since it was
concerned directly with us and was of significant size. A
few of the political prisoners had attended loosely organized meetings before this, but with the visit almost upon
us, all of us attended several serious meetings to thrash
out our alternatives. At these meetings, sharply contrast-
ing ideas were aired. Some thought the whole concept
fine, that we should cooperate with it, and hope for more
such occasions in the future; others did not like the idea
at all and suggested a boycott, being of the opinion that
the visitors should demonstrate; many were preoccupied
with the formal arrangements—if such and such happened,
what would we do, etc. If the conditions seemed too
stringent, some suggested a walkout, while others opted
for a sit-in, or the crossing of lines if set up.

In working out a response to the visit, a large part of
our problem was the result of poor communications between us and the organizers of the event. It was particularly vexing since our course of action ultimately depended upon the actions of the visitors. The organizers of

the visit were partly to blame for this lack of adequate communication, especially at that point at which we could have been told what was to happen but were not. We were, instead, left at the mercy of the prison administration, which was certainly not going to give us precise information. In the end, most of the political prisoners went to the religious service and visitation in the morning and to the entertainment in the afternoon: after visiting for ten minutes each with seven or eight successive busloads of people in the morning, and after Joan Baez sang in the afternoon, we were as confused as ever. However, the event at least brought the political prisoners together as an identifiable unit, more so than it had seemed to be before the day's festivities.

A few weeks later, in early January, 1969, a confrontation took place which centered around me and another political prisoner, Richard Chandler. Chandler had recently arrived at Allenwood and had been sporadically engaging in personal-witness, absolutist resistance. He had refused to shave and get a haircut; he had refused to do the orderly work assigned to him; at times, he would not be in the right place for the count. Finally, the administration put him under restrictions. He was not permitted to watch TV, go to the library, or leave his dormitory except for meals—which he could not eat in the dining hall but had to carry on a tray back to his quarters. He had to wash his own tray and silverware and his own clothing. We found the whole harassment procedure rather funny.

In the meantime, I was slowing down to almost a standstill on my work detail. At times, I would be either late for work or not show up not all, in which case the detail officer would have to come and get me. The work we were doing at the time was more galling than usual, being make-work (cutting brush and policing areas—i.e., picking up papers and debris). My thinking, like Chandler's, was centered around a personal revulsion toward the work I was doing. I was not, at the time, organization-oriented, and I had no specific goal in mind concerning the type of individual witness I was carrying on.

Things came to a head for both of us on January 6. I was called into the camp office and given a disciplinary hearing because of my poor work record. One of the questions put to me was whether or not I would report to work the next morning. I said: "perhaps." That was the only answer I would give and it was not acceptable. It was decided to send me back to the penitentiary. Chandler, too, was running into difficulty that same afternoon. He had tried to eat in the mess hall but had been rebuffed; he was called into the office immediately after me, and it was decided to send him back to the penitentiary too.

The procedure for going back to the penitentiary is supposedly a gentlemanly affair. The inmate returns to his dormitory, packs his belongings, lugs them up to the administration building, and is personally driven the sixteen miles back to the penitentiary by one of the hacks. But that wasn't the route that I had in mind. For some time previous, I had made up my mind that if I was going to be shipped back to the wall, they would have to carry me.

Chandler and I went back to our dormitories. It was 4:00 P.M.—count-time—which meant that the dormitories would be filled with inmates. I was pleased at the timing, because what I was about to do would be more effective before an audience. I spoke with a few political and nonpolitical prisoners and told them what was up. Word that we were being sent back to the penitentiary spread fast. Such an occurrence is a hot news item no matter to whom it happens. In addition, I told some political prisoners that I was not going to walk.

There soon came a call over the PA system requesting

our appearance at the administration building with our belongings. A hack appeared at the dormitory door and repeated the request. I told him, before numerous witnesses, that I would offer no resistance but that I was not going to go voluntarily. He called for reinforcements and I sat down on my bunk. Dan Kelly, another political prisoner, came and sat down with me. In a few minutes, five hacks arrived. There was a short dialogue as to whether I would walk and to whether Kelly was going to get out of the way: we both declined. The hacks grabbed hold of our legs and began to drag us out of the dormitory, our backs scraping the floor. The forty or so inmates there looked on.

When we reached the door, Alan Solomonow, yet another political prisoner, joined the fray by sitting down and attempting to block the doorway. He too was grabbed by the legs and dragged out the door, onto the sidewalk, and up toward the administration building. The distance from the dormitory to the administration building is just less than three hundred yards. The way was along a cement sidewalk and a loose-gravel parking lot. By this time, Chandler had decided to walk.

As the three of us, Kelly, Solomonow, and I were being dragged out of the doorway and onto the sidewalk, we were joined by most of the other political prisoners who stood around and tried to cajole the hacks into being gentler. Huffing and puffing, they refused, saying that we should get up and walk like men. After a short distance, the caravan stopped while the hacks caught their breath. All of us continued to talk to them, saying that it would be easier on them if they carried us instead. I recall that a number of political prisoners constantly berated the hacks and refused to return to their dormitories when told to. A few of them became vociferous when one of the hacks kicked Kelly in the butt and the small of the back while he lay on the pavement. The dragging started again and we were hauled the rest of the way to the administration building.

Meanwhile, the nonpolitical-prisoner population was not entirely removed from the affair. Almost the entire camp population was on hand since, as noted, it was count-time: they gathered at the entranceways of the three main dormitories and watched the event unfold. Almost all of them supported the political prisoners. For many reasons, it would not have been wise for them to join us and they did not. However, from out of the gathering of inmates looking on came numerous verbal jabs at the hacks—"you motherfuckers, you cocksuckers, you wouldn't kick someone who'd hit you back"—and so forth. There was one inmate whom I specifically recall having possibly mistaken the situation. He was nearly punched out by a group of nonpolitical prisoners after he had yelled encouragement to the hacks. Fortunately for him, he was already scheduled to leave the camp the next day.

I found out later that on the following day an old sheet was hung on the wall of a dormitory. On it was written the name of the hack who had kicked Kelly in the butt and following it were the words, "You wanted to kiss it, not kick it." Later that day the same hack was summarily run out of the dormitory by several inmates who said, "Yeah, there goes that motherfucker who kicked that kid."

When we finally made it to the administration building we saw that no one was badly hurt. (Solomonow did have burns and scrape marks on his back and buttocks where his shirt and pants had worn through from the dragging. I had had the foresight to wear my heavy winter coat, as did Kelly.) Chandler and I were then put in a car and driven to the penitentiary. To their surprise, Kelly, Solomonow, and several other political prisoners who had fol-

lowed us all the way were told that they could return to
their dormitories: for them, this particular confrontation
ended except for subsequent discussions with the administrative staff.

When Chandler and I arrived at the penitentiary, we
were made to stand for over two hours in a light snowfall
because we had refused to walk across the prison yard to
the cellblocks. We were finally carried and taken to the
strip room adjacent to the hole where we both refused to
strip. A couple of hacks then literally ripped our clothing
off our bodies, grabbed our feet, and dragged us, naked,
over thirty yards of cement flooring to two cells in the
hole. We spent the night there, in cells equipped with a
porcelain commode and sink and a steel-slab bunk, without mattress, blanket, or sheets. After a few hours, a pair
of pants and a shirt were thrown into each of our cells but
we did not wear them that night since we had learned that
there were two other men—nonpolitical prisoners—in the
hole who were being kept naked.

The next morning I put on my pants and undershirt and
was taken upstairs to one of the segregation cells. These
cells have a bed, mattress, blanket, sheets, and a locker, as
well as the usual toilet facilities. There is also a window
in each cell, unlike those in the hole which are entirely
closed. In a little while, Chandler was carried naked up
the stairs and also put into one of the segregation cells.

After another day in segregation, I thought it would be
a good idea to try to get back to Allenwood and get the
story out, and so I arranged for a meeting with the associate warden. I told him that I would be willing to go back
to work, if returned to Allenwood. He took the bait and
had me driven back that same evening: it seemed that
he thought that my returning to Allenwood immediately
might have a calming effect on the situation. Apparently,

the camp administration was genuinely shaken by the
events which had transpired a few days earlier. I was willing to let the associate warden think whatever he wanted.
Chandler decided to continue to refuse to work and he
was kept in segregation. I returned to Allenwood but not
for very long: three weeks later I was again taken back to
the penitentiary.

During these three weeks, I reported for work as scheduled but took to openly criticizing the futility of what we
were doing. The detail officer finally agreed with me, but
said, "After all, what is prison all about, you have to do
something to keep busy." He put me to work by myself
so that I wouldn't disturb the rest of the detail. My resistance was still of a personal nature, with no specific goal
in mind. But during these three weeks I had begun to
formulate a more organized approach to prison resistance.
In several informal rap sessions with various political prisoners, I brought up the idea of an inmate council to act
as representatives for the inmate population and to make
specific grievances known to the administration. I thought
that the political prisoners should become more involved
in the politics of the prison; I further thought that we
should get together and work to change present prison
conditions, without losing sight of the long-range goal of
abolishing prisons altogether. We had a large meeting and
I explained these ideas—some men agreed, some did not.
I told the assembled political prisoners that I was writing
up a proposal for an inmate council and that I was going
to submit it to the camp newspaper for publication. I
knew, of course, that the proposal would have to go
through the camp superintendent before it could be
printed.

Four days after this meeting and two days after I submitted the proposal, I was called into the office. The camp

superintendent said that the associate warden wanted to speak to me and that I was to go immediately to the penitentiary. I thought I smelled a rat but I decided to go voluntarily. Before I went, I spotted a couple of political prisoners, told them what was up, and expressed my apprehensions. When I got to the penitentiary, the rat showed his face and I was told that I was going to be kept inside the penitentiary. I was also taken before a good-time forfeiture board and put on trial: the charge against me was "continued poor institutional adjustment." One of my "crimes" was the writing up of the proposal for an inmate council after I'd been told by the camp superintendent to forget the idea. This was an outright lie: the camp superintendent had never told me not to write it up. It was obvious that my attempt to organize an inmate council was the primary reason for moving me from Allenwood.

I didn't return to Allenwood that evening and the political prisoners held an emergency meeting, the outcome of which was that twelve political prisoners refused to report to work the next morning. They demanded my return, the creation of an inmate council, and an end to involuntary servitude as preconditions to their returning to work: all twelve were returned to the penitentiary and placed in the segregation unit. In transit, one or two of them were roughed up. The twelve began a fast which included all solid foods and all beverages excepting water.

In the days and weeks that followed, we tried to get this story out. The only success we had was some mention in a few small-circulation peace publications. A prime difficulty during these days was my lack of opportunity to communicate with the fasting prisoners—I was in the main prison population and they were in administrative segregation. If I had decided to non-cooperate, I knew that I would not be sent in with them, but to some other section of the penitentiary. Our position was weak because we had not even begun to discuss such an action as the work stoppage and, further, we had not organized proper outside support. At that point we were effectively checkmated; gradually, over the course of about a month, one by one the political prisoners discontinued their fast and returned to work at Allenwood. I was never re-transferred to Allenwood. Several months later I was exiled to the Lewisburg Prison Farm Camp.

—DAVID MILLER

PETERSBURG FEDERAL REFORMATORY

There seems to be a general pattern in the Federal prison system of discrimination against Selective-Service violators in that they are often not allowed to participate in work- and study-release programs. At Petersburg Federal Reformatory, political prisoners were not even permitted to engage in vocational-training programs. There are exceptions, but as a general rule this pattern is followed. At Petersburg, there were *no* exceptions.

During the fall of 1968, Duncan Stout, a Selective-Service violator from Virginia, was sent to the reformatory for a ninety-day, pre-sentence observation period. After he had been at the reformatory for about a month, Stout's judge had him brought to his chamber for an interview. During this interview Stout mentioned the discrimination shown to political prisoners at the reformatory. The judge showed a great deal of interest and suggested that Stout write a letter to him asking for relief from the discriminatory practices: he said that he would regard the letter as a writ. Upon Stout's return to Petersburg he and I drafted a letter to the judge alleging that we were being denied access to vocational training and work- and study-release because of our status as political prisoners; we also stated that political prisoners were being denied permission to receive visits from or to correspond with clergymen.

Of the other nine political prisoners at the reformatory, only two would co-sign the letter. They gave various reasons for not signing it, the most common being that they were afraid that if they did, they might be denied parole. This fear was not unfounded, inasmuch as a week after we mailed the letter, the official in charge of discipline at the reformatory told me that if I did not discontinue my "organizing" activities I would be denied parole.

The judge considered the letter a writ under the All Writs Act and filed it on our behalf, naming the warden of the reformatory, the director of the Federal Bureau of Prisons, and the Attorney General of the United States as respondents. We first heard that the writ had been filed during a newscast on the local radio station. The story later received moderate attention in the local newspapers as well as in the *Washington Post*.

The date of the hearing was set for December 31, 1968, which gave us very little time to prepare our case. We were assigned a court-appointed lawyer but he didn't come to see us until four days before the hearing and was of no use to us whatsoever. Meanwhile, Stout was released on bail and I was placed in segregation for refusing to assist in the construction of a new prison building. (After the writ had been filed I was transferred from my rather plush job as a clerk in the infirmary to a much less coveted construction job.)

At the December 31 hearing the judge allowed the four of us to "represent all others similarly situated" and treated the suit as a class action. All of us took the stand and repeated our allegations. A Richmond, Virginia, clergyman testified that he had been told by the warden that he could not visit me because I was a Selective-Service violator. The assistant warden and two case-workers took the stand and denied that there was any discrimination against Selective-Service felons. They produced false documents which purported to indicate that four Selective-Service violators were enrolled in the vocational-training program. One of the four was not a Selective-Service violator, another was not and had never been enrolled in the vocational-training program, and the other two names, to the best of our knowledge, were fictitious. They admitted that no Selective-Service violators were enrolled in the study- or work-release program, but attributed this to its small size. They glibly glossed over the fact that the warden had told the clergyman that he could not visit me, and stated that they had mailed him a letter saying that he could: he never received the letter. So they lied. My case-worker even went so far as to deny that I had ever asked for vocational training or study-release. (I had asked for both on numerous occasions.) The judge stated that we had not presented sufficient evidence to support our allegations and dismissed the case. Nine days later all of us who had signed the letter were transferred from Petersburg Reformatory, split up, and sent to different institutions.

In retrospect, it is clear that we should have waited much longer before sending our letter to the judge; we should have carefully and methodically collected evidence and statements from all the other political prisoners at the institution; we should have made all our requests for training and work- or study-release in writing and should have kept copies of all such requests; finally, we should have had legions of clergymen request permission to correspond with and visit political prisoners.

Of course, even had we won, the most that probably would have happened is that the Federal prison system would have been forced to allow a token number of political prisoners to participate in the requested programs. The prison system is a subverter, not a respecter, of law and order.

—Donald C. Baty

We have described these incidents because we think that they give a fairly accurate picture of where political prisoners are in terms of resistance. Given our resources, the scope of the problem, and our purported commitment to revolutionary change, we are indeed at a low point. A monumental job awaits us, beginning with our self-organization and education, and continuing through a successful campaign to alter the programs and policies of the Federal Bureau of Prisons.

There are many obstacles, problems, and stumbling blocks in the path of the development of a radical political approach to prison reform. Before we can offer a program and direction for an organized, in-prison political movement, we must examine the major pitfalls which the political prisoners will face. The starting point is an appreciation and understanding of the differences between various categories and subgroupings of political prisoners themselves: they are not the homogeneous unit they are thought to be. The wide variety of personalities and political perspectives among them makes any organized activity a significant accomplishment. Thus, let us attempt to categorize the different types of political prisoners.

We must exclude at the outset groups like the Jehovah's

Witnesses, the Amish, and the Mennonite Brethren from the general classification "political prisoners." While we do not wish to include them, they are usually to be found wherever political prisoners are incarcerated, so a few words about them are in order.

The Jehovah's Witnesses or JW's, as they are often called, are the largest single group of Selective-Service violators in prison. You have probably seen them on street corners and they have knocked on your door on Sunday mornings. Perhaps you bought a copy of *Awake* or *Watchtower* in the hope that that would satisfy them and that they would go away: what you did not know is that once you bought a magazine, you were marked down in their record books as a target for a follow-up house call a week or two later. If the foot got further in the door the second time, home Bible-study sessions and a visit to the local Kingdom Hall would be persuasively suggested. If the unsuspecting householder (the term they use) gives way to these suggestions, he, she, or the entire family is well on the way to conversion and subsequent membership in the "world's fastest-growing religion." The JW's have perfected a selling technique that is the envy of the sales industry; they spend hours upon hours of meeting-time—in and out of prison—going over the techniques and strategy that will bring a householder from initial contact to final conversion.

Many political prisoners come to prison and to the farm camps knowing little of the JW's. But there almost always is a latent fear that every morning one will be awakened by a young man bringing the "truth that shall make you free." Fortunately we can put that fear to rest: the JW's do not proselytize in prison as they do on the street. They will convert an inmate if he wishes, but their religious activity is confined to their own meetings, some four or five a week. By some form of theological gymnastics, in prison they hold in abeyance their absolute command to build Jehovah's Kingdom. The reason, of course, is that in a confined prison situation, other prisoners would not stand for it.

The JW's look at the world through apocalyptic lenses. Their message is summed up nicely in their initial pitch. The world is in a state of chaos—wars and rumors of wars! Wouldn't you rather live in a world where the lamb lay down with the lion, and (not stated but implicit) where those vexing decisions about a changing world need not bℓ made? If yes, then come, take up your *Watchtower* and be free.

Personally, the JW's are friendly and pleasant; they are easy to get along with; they cause no ripples; they are the most trustworthy inmates a prison could have. For this reason, some inmates, including some political prisoners, do not trust them. Then again, because the JW's theoretically are always supposed to tell the truth, it may be wise not to confide details of one's prison activities to them. Many prisoners suspect that they are snitches—and indeed, some are. Most, however, learn that it is safer to lie. It has been our experience that political discussions with them prove fruitless: they are too well indoctrinated. There may be one or two exceptions but for the most part one's time is better spent elsewhere.

The Selective-Service violators from the Amish and Mennonite communities are part of these famous Dutch-German peace churches. They are classic conscientious objectors. They are not apocalyptic but they are as anti-intellectual and apolitical as the JW's. Quiet, easygoing chaps, and good farmers, they are the only prisoners allowed to have beards and bushy hair in deference to their religious convictions. Those few in prison and at Allenwood seem to be there as a result of an inane Federal court in Ohio.

The Muslim Selective-Service violators do their time as well as any other group; they stick together and make a practice of not arguing with whites, while they quietly try to interest their black brothers in their beliefs.

Next are the political prisoners. Within the political-prisoner grouping there exist wide varieties of opinion on every serious question: politics, religion, tactics, violence, nonviolence, life style, etc. We have found that political prisoners who are interested in organizing have underestimated these differences. We do not mean to suggest that we are at one another's throats: but it is necessary to understand that twenty-five to thirty men together in prison because of their anti-war beliefs do not necessarily make up a cohesive political force.

There are political prisoners of a nonpacifist ideology who have taken a hard anti-imperialist line against the government of the United States and against the war in Vietnam in particular. These prisoners have often consciously made good use of the mass media, the courts, and their organizational talents to contribute to the anti-war movement.

Others, of a pacifist ideology, are usually of an anarchist bent as well. Their pacifist public stand is expressed in the hope of influencing other people, while at the same time, they are making a personal moral witness.

Some prisoners, of a pacifist ideology, have eschewed all publicity. They—literally—are doing their own thing. They want no part of a movement; they would prefer that the government leave them alone; they may use "mind-blowing" agents, and they are likely to be interested in free communities on the land and in the city.

Finally, there are political prisoners who did not challenge the draft but who would have accepted conscientious-objector status if it were given them. They were denied this status, and when the time came for induction, they refused to go.

Apart from the different beliefs that brought these men to prison, there is an overriding air of independence even among the more politically oriented political prisoners. This independence has a stunting effect on in-prison organizing. Indeed, many political prisoners, even when politically conscious, seem suspicious of organized activity; they are often unwilling or unable to make the kind of compromises necessary for effective political activity; there is an infectious prejudice for "going it alone." Of monumental importance is the fact that many political prisoners balk at identifying themselves as such in the first place and refuse to come to in-prison political gatherings. This attitude quite effectively cuts organizational and concerted action short. Often, even when organized resistance is broached, there are political prisoners who militate against the tactically reformist approach that is necessary if prison resistance is to carry us beyond the point of solitary witness. They are so opposed to the entire conceptual basis for prison that they see little relevance in taking any practical steps to change prison conditions short of abolishing all prisons, scarcely a serious possibility at the present time.

Among political prisoners there is a serious flaw involving decision-making processes, since there is no hierarchy of power, elected or assumed. Positions and plans of action are arrived at by consensus: those sharply disagreeing simply leave the group. The lack of a disciplined political unit where each man is obliged to abide by the decisions of a group makes political activity that much more difficult.

They differ substantially on questions involving tactics.

In this area, what may or may not be moral for specific political prisoners is a factor that must be contended with. Tactically, some political prisoners have difficulty in confronting the enemy because they refuse to think in terms of the existence of enemies.

It is not surprising, then, that organized resistance by political prisoners has run into problems. Bringing political prisoners together for resistance and in-prison political activity is a job which requires patience and hard work. If we are to get even so far as to *begin* to confront the prison authorities on a systematic basis, political prisoners must significantly resolve and dispose of many of the divisive traits outlined above.

It may well be that as the government is forced to assume a more repressive position regarding political dissenters, the proportion of political prisoners will shift in favor of politically conscious individuals. Were this to happen some of the existing problems might be obviated. In other words, as the government begins to crack down on white college students, black radicals, and full-time Movement organizers, the proportion of individualistic political prisoners may decrease. Whether, of course, the new breed of political prisoners can overcome their own mutual distrust of one another is a crucial but unanswerable question for now.

We have earlier noted that there is an argument against identification of political prisoners with one another: it runs something like this. Identification as a distinct group is elitist and tends to undermine solidarity with other prisoners who, in a wider sense of the term, are political prisoners themselves. To emphasize *our* status as political prisoners is seemingly to ask to be treated differently from other prisoners—that would drive deeper the wedge of hostility between us and the nonpolitical prisoners.

We do not agree with that argument. We must begin with the basic question: "Are we or are we not—objectively—political prisoners?" The answer is that we *are*. The government refuses to recognize the existence of political prisoners: it is incumbent upon us to refuse, in turn, to be relegated to anonymity. By demanding recognition as political prisoners, we can go a long way toward destroying this government's democratic façade. Further, we have found no evidence to support the contention that group identification tends to undermine solidarity with other inmates. In fact, we have found the opposite to be true. On the few occasions when political prisoners resisted prison authority in an open and concerted fashion, their stock, in the eyes of nonpolitical prisoners, was never so high. Correspondingly, the more dispersed our efforts, the more open we were to the barbs and criticisms of our fellow inmates.

To say that we are political prisoners is not to ask for special privileges. It is clear that since political prisoners are part of a larger prison community, any demands for better treatment must be made on behalf of *all* prisoners. We can make such demands and make them most effectively from an organized base.

Actually, it is a little spurious for some political prisoners to say that they do not want special privileges and treatment: most have already accepted special status from prison authorities since all are almost automatically sent to minimum-security farm camps soon after imprisonment. In no way can a political prisoner deny that he has accepted special privilege by accepting incarceration at the farm camps. Most prisoners never set foot on a farm camp. If moral consistency is at stake we can do nothing less than admit that tacitly, at least, the government does treat us specially.

Organized resistance aside, there is a necessity for and inevitability in political prisoners identifying with one another, since the reality of the situation is that they must either identify with one another or with no one at all. We just do not fit anywhere else, and although we can and do relate to other prisoners, that relatedness starts with self-identity.

To look at it in another way: when a political prisoner says that he does not want to identify himself as such but rather as part of the wider prison community what in fact is he talking about? There is no wider prison community that we know about. There is the black community, the Spanish-speaking community, the Jewish community, the Italian community, the "hillbilly" community, etc. Political prisoners just will *not* be accepted as authentic elements of any of these communities. The only way for one to fit into any given group (and it cannot be accomplished with all of them) is for the political prisoner to completely forsake his individual political identity. For example, if a Jewish political prisoner wanted to identify with Jewish inmates, he would have to associate with and acquire all the prejudices of these inmates while excluding himself from *all other* inmate groupings. Then, and only then, might he be accepted as part of the Jewish community. It of course then follows that the whole idea of solidarity with all inmates is negated by the restrictions of Jewish identity— the political prisoner is right back where he started, only, we fear, worse off. With very few exceptions, notably with black and Spanish-speaking political prisoners, an attempt to identify with any group except one's own will prove futile at best.

Another major problem that faces those interested in organized political activity in prison is the question of whether or not political prisoners should accept the privilege of the minimum-security farm camps. There are several arguments for and against this.

The arguments for staying in the penitentiary are as follows: the farm camps are on the fringe of prison activity. The life of the institution, good or bad, passes by the farm camps almost completely. The bulk of the prison population—and the most interesting part of it—is in the penitentiary. The farm camps are populated by those inmates who are the most cooperative. That means that the most angry, dissident, and recalcitrant inmates, the natural allies for resistance, are behind the walls and not at the farm camps. What is more, the greatest injustices take place behind the wall and if we are to organize around these issues, we have to be there.

The arguments for going to the farm camps are: the farm camp has a freer and easier atmosphere than the penitentiary; regulations are more relaxed; the pressures of confinement are not as great as they are at the penitentiary; visiting procedures are more flexible; censorship of books and periodicals is less stringent; if it is one's choice to study and do the easiest possible time, the farm camps are far better than the penitentiary. In terms of organized resistance, some feel that it might be tactically better to accept the privilege of the farm camps and resist from there. This approach would of course challenge the liberal pretensions of the farm camp setup, although it must be admitted that most inmates would gladly settle for these liberal pretensions if it meant that they could get out from under the oppressiveness of the penitentiary. Whatever the limitations of the farm camps—and they are many— life there is far better than it is behind the wall. There is a significant doubt as to the ability of a number of political prisoners to deal with and psychologically survive penitentiary life. The naïveté and indecision that characterize some political prisoners makes it unwise for them to stay in the penitentiary: for them, good sense alone dictates that they ought to remain at the camps.

Our recommendation to prospective political prisoners is that they must weigh the alternatives and make their own decision. A major consideration would be that the novice political prisoner ought to go where he will find the largest number of his fellows if, that is, the administration is willing to send him there. If the majority of political prisoners is at the farm camps, that would be his best bet. One can always "find his way back" to the penitentiary if, later, that becomes his choice. On the other hand, if the majority of cadre is at the penitentiary, it might be better to stay there and add to the constituency. One point should be mentioned: there is little advantage for the isolated political prisoner in deciding to stay within the penitentiary. Group support is needed; the odds against the solitary political prisoner are probably too great to beat.

There is a related problem to the farm camp question. There are (usually unreliable) rumors that the prison authorities are preparing to set aside several camps for the exclusive habitation of political prisoners: Allenwood has been mentioned as one site, Safford, Arizona as another. If the rumors become reality, some basic elements of our analysis would require revision. However, in itself, we have no reason to fear such a move. If political prisoners do not like the arrangement, there is an easy way to be returned to a penitentiary in order to re-establish contact with nonpolitical prisoners. A unified refusal to work will do the trick.

There is one indication which points to the suspicion that the Bureau of Prisons will not set up camps for the exclusive use of political prisoners. If the government did move in that direction, it would then have to admit to the

existence of political prisoners, an admission we do not
think it is ready to make. We feel that the policy of the
government will continue to be much the same as it has
been with, perhaps, some quantitative change. There may
be several camps around the country that will house political *and* nonpolitical prisoners, though there will be a
large percentage of political prisoners, conceivably even
a majority at some camps. The prison authorities will continually strive to weed out of those camps with high political-prisoner concentrations those among them who are
considered to be organizers: these inmates will be spread
thin and, hopefully, isolated within the prison system. Indeed, this systematic weeding-out process is already in effect. At any given time, one can expect to find three
political prisoners at Lewisburg Farm Camp. The three invariably are thought of by prison administrators as agitators or organizers. For example, for one six-month period
in 1968, political prisoners Baty, Levy, and Miller were the
only ones to be found at Lewisburg. Donald Baty was
thought of as an organizer because he filed a writ against
the prison authorities while at Petersburg Reformatory.
The authors [David Miller and Howard Levy] were
thought of as organizers because of their activities at
Allenwood Farm Camp and the USDB, respectively. The
very day that Levy was released from Lewisburg his place
was taken by a new political prisoner, George Vlasits, an
organizer for the now-defunct Southern Student Organizing Committee (SSOC).

Before embarking upon a program of resistance, political prisoners must assess their strengths and weaknesses
as well as the strengths and weaknesses of the enemy. The
administration has its weapons and we have ours. The administration banks heavily on the prejudices of American
society. The law-and-order mentality has deep roots and
vicious men continually fan the embers of bias against the

"criminal element." In communities surrounding prisons, the staff of the prison consciously and unconsciously projects itself as the "thin blue line" that separates the unsuspecting public from the ravaging criminals in the penitentiary. The administration has all the powers we have previously described in the chapter on punishment. It can beat prisoners into submission with overwhelming firepower and military advantage; it can take away good time and parole; it can bring additional criminal charges; and leaders of resistance can be shuffled from one institution to another.

It also comes equipped with miles of bureaucratic red tape. Every poor soul along the line weeps and bemoans his fate as one who must carry out the orders of his superiors. Through censorship and controlled visiting, the administration has near-absolute control over the flow of vital information from inside the prison to the outside world. The administration operates best in darkness and a shroud of mystery.

But political prisoners are not without weapons of their own. They can expose the prison system as the cruel and vindictive instrument it is, by juxtaposing its liberal, rehabilitative pretensions against the reality of its practices and effect. As a rule, they have a sound moral integrity that acts as a damper on the lying and false charges of the administration. Very importantly, political prisoners have good resources in regard to the mass media: they are newsworthy and can use the media to their advantage. Potentially, they have good financial, legal, and organizational support outside of prison. Transforming this potential support into active support is admittedly another matter. They are fairly well versed in civil disobedience, primarily of the nonviolent type, and have had experience in leading and managing demonstrations. Finally, the authorities are a clear enemy whom, theoretically, *all* prisoners oppose.

Most of us agree that for in-prison resistance to be effective we must incorporate nonpolitical prisoners into our movement. Up until now, this has not been tried—we have not yet organized ourselves!

The final question regarding prison resistance is whether or not it is worthwhile. Are the risks too great? Is there any chance of success? What, if any, are the political and social values of resistance?

While the particulars defy generalization we should enumerate the political and social values of prison resistance.

1. Prison resistance aids the political development of those partaking in it. It is a process of self-education in itself and complements more formal intellectual pursuits.

2. Prison resistance is helpful and perhaps crucial in maintaining group morale and solidarity.

3. Prisons represent the bedrock of our oppressive society and we cannot afford to ignore the prison system if we propose to relate to the victims of this society.

4. The prison system provides backing for other repressive agencies within this society, such as the police and the military. To attack the one is to attack them all.

5. The publicity accompanying prison resistance will help to demystify prisons, thus removing some of the fear from the minds of potential radical activists, as well as help provide a deterrent against a possible increase in ill-treatment of prisoners.

6. A continuation of their political activity in prison will help political prisoners maintain their roles as political activists, especially if good lines of communication are maintained. In this way the repressive effect of prison will be lessened.

Chapter 18 WORK

In Federal and military prisons, all inmates, including political prisoners, are compelled to work.

Operating a prison is a complicated affair. Prisons are "total institutions" in that they comprise self-contained and nearly self-sufficient communities unto themselves. For inmates, contact with the outside world is minimal and for that reason the institution must provide for all of the inmates' needs—food, shelter, rest, health, recreation, etc. And, since prisons are often located in small, isolated towns, the prison staff also finds it difficult to escape the totality of the institution: as a consequence, many of their needs must also be satisfied by the institution.

The myriad tasks involved in operating a total institution occupy the attention of many hundreds of individuals. An average Federal prison with a daily census of 1,800 prisoners employs approximately 350 men and women. These full-time, paid employees are concerned with administrative, security, and supervisory tasks. But without the cooperation and assistance of the inmates it is doubtful that such a prison could function at peak efficiency unless the number of non-prisoner employees were doubled or even tripled. While this, of course, could be accomplished, the expense of operating such a prison would be increased accordingly. Since the Federal government is notably parsimonious when the welfare of its society's ingrates are at stake, it is very likely that services would be curtailed and that, in the end, only the prisoners would be the real losers. Prisoners are thus given a Hobson's choice: either work as slave laborers or, if they refuse, suffer both immediate punishment and long-range deprivation of services.

Since the primary function of prison work is the maintenance and support of the institution, it is logical to find
that most work details revolve around institution-centered
needs. Hence, all prisons provide employment in diverse
tasks such as carpentry, plumbing, house painting, grounds
maintenance, electrical work, light construction, launder-
ing, kitchen work, barbering, and tailoring. If the prison
happens to be a farm camp, much of the work necessarily
deals with farming and the care, breeding, milking, slaugh-
tering, and butchering of animals. Every institution is also
able to provide a small number of prison "white collar"
jobs. Prison clerks are utilized in many departments; medical and dental technicians and aides are employed in the
hospital and clinics; inmate teachers and librarians are to
be found in the education department; and prisoners also
staff the prison newspaper, magazine, and radio station.

In addition to those jobs which directly serve the institution itself, most prisons also offer industrial jobs which
do not or only indirectly service the institution. In Federal
prisons, most of these jobs are organized under the aegis
of the Federal Prison Industries (FPI). FPI is a government corporation which is separate from the Federal
Bureau of Prisons, but which maintains manufacturing
plants on the premises of most Federal prisons. FPI was
incorporated some decades ago with seed money appropri-
ated by Congress. It was Congress's intent that FPI serve
as a rehabilitative tool by providing useful employment
skills which prisoners could subsequently put to use following their release from prison.

FPI is a profit-making venture, and in its years of existence has poured tens of millions of dollars worth of profit
back to the Treasury Department. A small portion of its
profits have been re-invested into FPI itself in order to ex-
pand plant facilities and to modernize equipment. Its

products include metal bunk beds, chairs, tables, cabinets, office furniture, shelfs, lockers, mattresses, blankets, sheets, pillow cases, shoes, and clothing. These items are sold to the Federal Bureau of Prisons and make up most of the furnishings of the prison system as well as most of the prison population's clothing. Some of the items are sold to other branches of the government, including the military. It should be noted that aside from the money which is re-invested into FPI, none of this corporation's profits are channeled back into the prison system.

FPI's balance sheet would be in the black if only because it is assured a safely controlled and predictable marketplace for its standardized products. But its profits skyrocket because its employees (with the exception of supervisors) are exploited prisoners who perform hard work for minuscule wages. Salaries for prisoner employees of FPI are graded according to time spent on the job, proficiency, and personal financial need, but add up to only between seventeen and thirty-six cents an hour. All other prisoners are, of course, workers and are paid no salary, but some can receive a "meritorious pay" allowance of ten dollars a month after they have been working at a particular job for six months.

FPI does not maintain a branch at the USDB, but at that institution some industrial jobs are available anyway. The most efficient income-producing operation at the USDB is a silk-screen plant which, like FPI, manufactures products, chiefly automobile bumper decals, which are sold at a profit to military bases throughout the world. In addition, the USDB operates various shops which directly service the needs of the institution's employees. Such services include appliance and TV repair, barbering, and engraving. Then too, high-ranking USDB officers illegally use the facilities of still other shops to have work performed for them at no cost. During the holiday season, the USDB printing shop does a thriving but non-remunerative business printing greeting cards and invitations for staff members, and occasionally for military cronies of staff members who are stationed at other military posts. Indeed, throughout the year the printing and silk-screen shops are called upon to print rather elaborate multicolored jobs for various fraternal and "patriotic" organizations to which staff members or their friends belong. One such job is for a certificate which was labeled "The American Patriotism Award." The irony of military prisoners, many of whom have committed trivial offenses, being illegally forced to goldbrick for "true blue" super-American-patriot superior officers is too rich in significance to go without passing comment.

Political prisoners, like all other prisoners, are, as we have said, forced to work. Again, as is true for all prisoners, they are afforded—provided they are on nobody's "shit list"—some option as to the type of work they wish to perform. In most prisons, the novice prisoner is assigned automatically, shortly after his arrival, to work in the kitchen or mess hall for anywhere from two to eight weeks. Following this initiation rite, the inmate is given an opportunity to meet with the Job Classification Board to indicate his job preference. Prisoners who have some prior job skill can often be fitted into a job where such skills can be utilized.

Unfortunately, full utilization of a prisoner's employment assets is less certain for those who are either highly skilled or whose skills are of a professional nature. Thus, doctors, dentists, lawyers, engineers, chemists, etc., are not permitted to practice their profession. And some prison administrators are reluctant to employ political prisoners in certain "sensitive" job slots such as education, radio broadcasting, and prison publishing. The explanation which is offered for these restrictions is that political prisoners are prone to propagandize for their political beliefs and all platforms ought be denied them. Such fears reach hysterical proportions at the USDB. Prison officials at some other institutions are less fearful of the "Red Peril" and may employ some political prisoners in these jobs. In reality, since all work activities are carefully monitored, fears in this regard are quite unfounded.

If, however, the fears of some prison officials seem irrational, perhaps it is worthwhile to speculate upon other unspoken reasons for the frequent underemployment of political prisoners. It is quite possible that some prison officials are unwilling to offer political prisoners professionally oriented assignments because such employment might enhance the image and prestige of political prisoners among the general inmate population. This would certainly have been the case had prison officials at the USDB agreed to one of the authors' [H.L.'s] request to allow him to work as a physician. Yet another, less likely though not altogether improbable explanation, relates to prison officials' own sense of insecurity and inadequacy. The fact is that some political prisoners can out-teach, out-write, and out-intellectualize most prison officials and the latter are understandably hesitant to expose themselves to the competition of more highly educated political prisoners.

In a few Federal prisons (i.e., Petersburg Reformatory, Virginia), political prisoners are denied employment in FPI. But this is not generally the case and the fact that relatively few political prisoners work for FPI is accounted for by the fact that political prisoners find factory labor unattractive. It is true that officials do not encourage political prisoners to work for FPI but this is probably a reflection of the biases of their political wards. On the other hand, a few of the brighter administrators may intuit, even if political prisoners do not, that a prison factory job may provide fertile soil for political agitation inasmuch as the prison factory worker is the prison system's exploited proletariat par excellence. Poor work conditions, low pay, and niggardly benefits are made to order and could provide grist for any radical's mill. Indeed, not long ago, FPI workers at Lewisburg Federal Penitentiary went on strike. As could be expected, class solidarity was not much in evidence, and the leaders of the strike were promptly isolated and soon shipped to other prisons. Nonetheless, the political potential is very real and even the somewhat aborted Lewisburg strike packed sufficient punch to benefit and win concessions for the remaining FPI employees there.

Every prison work detail is overseered by a detail supervisor. Supervisors are employed by the prison but are often quite insistent that they be differentiated from the guard personnel. Generally speaking, detail supervisors try to develop good rapport with their workers. It would seem that they conceive of themselves in one of two roles: either as a Big Brother to the younger inmates, or else as "one of the gang" as they relate to the older inmate population. These men are master boondogglers and have developed that art to near perfection. Their own indolence, together with their desire to be accepted by the inmates, means that they are not usually strict disciplinarians. Thus, they expect prisoners to work only halfheartedly and intermittently at that. Were detail supervisors to crack the whip this would give rise to open dissension among their prisoner-workers and this, in turn, would result in requests for job transfers which, more often than not, would be granted. However, since detail supervisors know that "boat rocking" is taboo for Federal government employees, it is in their interest to minimize friction by allowing prisoners to work at a leisurely and at times almost unnoticeable pace.

Despite the foregoing remarks, we do not wish to create the illusion that no work is demanded from inmates in Federal prisons, and even less do we wish to foster the idea that job overseers are really "good guys." The day-to-day operation and functioning of a prison depend in large measure on prisoner productivity, and therefore a certain inescapable amount of work must be performed each day. The prisoner who is completely unproductive will be pressured by his detail supervisor to shape up; should he continue with his desultory work habits he will be subject to a disciplinary report written by his supervisor. Of course, the loafer is also on the receiving end of criticism from his fellow inmates. If one man refuses to pull his share of the load, it only means that everyone else has to work that much harder. The prison staff is adept at playing off one worker against another, and loafers often find themselves in extremely untenable positions.

Aside from the fact that work supervisors can write disciplinary reports on workers and thus, in effect, send them to the hole, another aspect of their duties militates against any real rapport between them and the prisoners. To justify their own jobs, detail supervisors must always be in a position to demand work from their workers. Days simply cannot be allowed to pass with everyone just sitting on his butt. To fill the empty days when no real work needs to be done, "make-work" is created. Make-work in prison is important because there are far too many prisoners for the too few real jobs that exist. In the penitentiary, make-work usually centers on extra and useless cleaning of one facility or another. At farm camps, extra cleaning is also a form of make-work but it assumes other forms as well, such as brush clearing, or tearing down a fence (or some other structure) and rebuilding a similar structure some distance away. At times, it may be quite difficult to find work to do and supervisors have to go far out of their way in order to keep the prisoners occupied. One crew at the Lewisburg Farm Camp spent one whole week smoothing out a rutted road in the middle of a wheat field in the dead of winter. All such make-work is staunchly defended by the Calvinistically oriented prison administration. Furthermore, officials tend to deflect criticisms of superfluous work by ascribing these unfavorable attitudes to the laziness, recalcitrance, and criminality of the complaining inmate.

Most political prisoners have adopted a diffident but distantly friendly attitude toward their job supervisors. These men are much too low on the penal totem pole for political prisoners to be excessively troubled and confrontations with them are likely to produce only misery for these prisoners, as well as for the other men on the work crew, without any concomitant political reward.

Some political prisoners still feel that politica
sions with supervisors are worthwhile and will presumably lead to the disaffection of these prison employees. The authors have seen no evidence to support this supposition and view it, in our less charitable moments, as an exercise in naïveté. (There has been, in our experience, one exception to the foregoing. At the USDB, some of the mil itary police were won over to the side, at least in spirit, of the political prisoners. However, even this limited success involved only non-career MP's, and these men were there fore not at all equivalent to Federal-prison careerists.) One important defect in engaging supervisors in lengthy dis-- cussions is that other prisoners distrust anyone who assumes too friendly an attitude to any prison employee. This, together with the fact that job supervisors are in fre-

quent communication with administrators to whom they will inform on political prisoners in order to earn "brownie points" for themselves, should be borne in mind and weighed against the extreme unlikelihood that supervisors can be converted to radical positions.

The best way to deal with detail supervisors is to do the work to which one is assigned with about the same degree of efficiency and diligence exhibited by the average workers on the crew. On every crew, there can be observed a few persons who are overly industrious. Some prisoners work hard and keep busy either because they wish to give a good impression or because they do their time better that way. They say it is tougher to sit around and loaf than it is to go ahead and get the job done. This pattern is, for example, frequently followed by the Jehovah's Witnesses. The result of their diligence, however, is that the detail supervisor will invariably foist a greater and greater share of the work load onto the backs of his few exemplary workers; so that although enthusiastic workers please supervisors and staff, these workers receive no reward—except, of course, more work. Detail supervisors do make monthly reports to prison officials concerning the quality of their underlings' work, and these reports are forwarded to parole hearings. It is the broad consensus of many knowledgeable prisoners that such reports have little or no bearing upon the prospect of receiving or being denied parole. This would certainly seem to be even more true for political prisoners.

Most prisoners complain about work, but if the truth were ascertainable it is probable that even if work were not mandatory, most prisoners would choose it anyway. Whatever its defects, work fulfills one important function in prison: it consumes time. For inmates who are not intellectually inclined, boredom is an ever-present reality, and even the dullest prison job is preferable to unlimited leisure time. Political prisoners are different in some respects from other prisoners but the differences should not be magnified out of proportion. Though they tend to be more intellectual and more successfully able to deal with leisure time, it is doubtful that most political prisoners would know what to do with themselves if they were given the option of declining *all* work assignments.

It is well-nigh impossible to offer prospective political prisoners advice concerning which prison jobs will prove, if not rewarding, then least distasteful, since personal needs and predilections vary so greatly from individual to individual. We have, however, noted that when they have been made available to them, political prisoners have found some rewards working within the education, medical, dental, and chapel sections in work as instructors, technicians, or clerks. These jobs are somewhat fulfilling because they assist, if only slightly, one's fellow prisoners, although the end result of these efforts is at best a mixed blessing. These work sections, however, offer the additional benefit of providing a quiet and subdued atmosphere together with an abundance of free time, thus allowing the worker ample opportunity for reading, writing, and discussion. We have, however, known political prisoners who preferred to work outdoors and who enjoyed farm labor. Still others with mechanical aptitudes gravitate to machine, tool-and-die, printing, and woodworking shops.

Future political prisoners should understand that prison work differs in several major respects from non-prison work. This is the case even though prisoners generally work the usual eight-hour day (often from 8:00 A.M. to 4:00 P.M. with a half-hour off for lunch), and while on the job perform most of the tasks which a similar non-prison job might demand. Perhaps the most noticeable difference between prison and non-prison work is the enormous amount of manpower squandered in prison work. Many work crews employ ten men where three might be adequate. Work crews must be padded because there is not enough useful work to go around. Thus, no less than three "houseboys" serve the warden of Lewisburg Federal Penitentiary, while another three men are permanently employed during spring, summer, and fall tending the warden's garden. The warden's (and his family's) needs are many since he resides in a fifteen-room house resting on a very ample plot of land atop a hill overlooking his entire dominion—the prison plantation. Associate wardens have smaller but far from inadequate houses tended by only one houseboy; thus, the pecking order is clearly established. To be sure the houseboys are kept busy with their menial tasks; they are required to clean house, polish floors, wash, hang, and iron the clothes, cook the food, and wash the dishes—as well as do the baby sitting. This arrangement has the advantage—for the warden's and associate wardens' wives—of freeing them for more important duties: bridge, social teas, and poolside sunbathing at the prison's clubhouse, which is, incidentally, also maintained and serviced by prisoner labor.

Unlike non-prison workers, inmates are not permitted to wander from their job area to another entirely separate area, nor are they permitted to use the inter-institution telephone unless given authorization to do so. The non-ambulatory rule is not always strictly enforced but an offender is occasionally given a disciplinary report for "being out of place." Understandably, given the nature of prison-farm work, this rule is less applicable to the farm camps.

Again, unlike most non-prison jobs, a prisoner has no access to grievance committees—to say nothing of labor unions—to insure that his rights are protected. If he has a beef he may, at times, discuss it with his detail supervisor,

but this action is far from ideal. Most often, work problems are ignored and tolerated as well as possible. Indeed,
unlike most workers, the prisoner is not afforded an opportunity to freely contract his labor power; rather, he has it
taken away from him by prison authorities who have the
right to dispense with it as they see fit.

Finally, while the civilian worker may annually take a
vacation and thus escape the tedium of his work, the prisoner's one-week annual vacation is less satisfactory. While
on "vacation" the prisoner can travel only so far as his
dormitory or cell block and in reality this vacation, like all
the rest of his time, belongs to the "company." To see the
same faces day in and day out while at work or on vacation serves to re-emphasize the psychological and physical
totality of one's isolation. Therefore, attempts to escape
from the reality of prison through work or alternatively,
the reality of prison work through vacations, leads in both
instances to the same cul-de-sac.

Inasmuch as prison work comprises one-third of the
prisoner's time it is appropriate to consider an overview of
the entire prison employment situation. As we have noted,
the overwhelming majority of prison jobs exists to facili-
tate the operation of the prison itself. Given this para-
mount need, can prison employment offer the inmate any
substantial benefits other than the miserable salary which
he may receive and the extra good time which he may ac-
cumulate as a reward for satisfactory job performance?
(The extra good time usually ranges from two to five days
per month, depending upon the length of time on the job,
and, much less importantly, the ratings the prisoner receives on his detail supervisor's monthly reports.) If prison
officials are to be believed, prison work is a major rehabilitative tool in that it equips prisoners for employment upon
their release from prison. In the euphemistic parlance of

prison administrators, detail supervisors are referred to as "correctional supervisors" whose mission it is to provide vocational training to each inmate and help the inmate develop "good work habits."

The truth is that only an insignificant minority of prisoners ever uses the job skills which are learned in prison after release. And in view of the fact that a high percentage of Federal prisoners now serving time are likely to be reconfined again for another stint following their release it is safe to conclude that prison work programs are, in terms of rehabilitation, abject failures.

Prison work fails to rehabilitate men because inmates are forced to perform work for which they have scant interest, enthusiasm, or aptitude. (The spectacle of long-time urban dwellers driving tractors or milking cows is greeted with wry amusement by officials and prisoners alike.) Rehabilitation fails because far too many prison jobs, though necessary for the maintenance of the prison, require no skill and represent dead-end employment options on the street. Prisons do need dishwashers, floor sweepers, custodians, clerks, groundskeepers, etc., but few prisoners are prepared, after release, to give up "criminal activities" for such blind-alley employment pursuits.

Prison work fails because little effort is expended to correlate prison jobs with the type of skills private industry demands, and the sluggish prison bureaucracy is ill-suited to adjust its programs to meet the dynamically changing needs of the private sector of the economy. Finally, prison work fails because the entire prison experience subjects prisoners to intense psychological tension which engenders feelings of frustration, degradation, and humiliation. Such pressures would tend to subvert even an *ideal* rehabilitation program. Rather than encouraging "good work habits" the exploitative characteristics of prison work

alienate inmates from work experience. At the heart of
the matter is a philosophical difference over the question
of the purpose of prison work. Prison work can be used as
an instrument of punishment or as a rehabilitative tool.
Unfortunately, even progressive prison administrators have
not thought the matter through and do not comprehend that punishment and rehabilitation are mutually antagonistic goals. The long history of prison work as punishment, from the rock pile to the chain gang, needs no detailing here. While the emphasis has been slowly changing
in recent years it is unmistakably clear that the contradic-
tion between punishment and rehabilitation still exists
and that, if anything, work as punishment still carries
the day.

In the case of political prisoners the concept of work as
punishment is a surety. Prison authorities freely and
openly admit that rehabilitation of political prisoners is
not even a tangential goal. Political prisoners must work
not because their welfare demands as much, but because
there simply is no way to keep them occupied and out of
the way while at the same time punishing them to the
maximum. While at the Lewisburg Farm Camp, two political prisoners submitted a proposal to the prison authorities, demanding a half-day work schedule for all prisoners
who wished to undertake their own self-study program.
The thrust behind the demand was that for some prisoners, most notably but not exclusively political prisoners, such self-study sessions would be more akin to self-
advancement than a full work schedule milking cows or
mowing lawns could ever be. Prison officials turned
thumbs down on the proposal.

Of course, "progressive" American penologists would
deny the allegation that prison work is nothing more than
a method of punishment. Federal prison administrations

are ever ready to publicly display what we term their "showcase" work project. At Lewisburg Federal Penitentiary, officials are inordinately proud of their on-the-job training program for dental technicians. At the USDB, as well as at several Federal penitentiaries, the showcase feature is an IBM computer program. Other examples could be cited, but no detailed survey is required inasmuch as these programs invariably reach out only to a tiny number of prisoners and are almost surely initiated to foster the public image of prisons as institutions dedicated to the high-sounding principle of rehabilitation. At the present time, we can see no possibility that these programs will be expanded to encompass the majority, or for that matter, more than one or two per cent of the total prison population.

A word or two concerning the attitudes of political prisoners to prison work as these attitudes relate to prison resistance will complete this chapter. All political prisoners appreciate the utter wastefulness and inconsequence of prison work. Until now, most political prisoners have accepted work assignments both as a relief from the tedium of what often seems to be an infinity of time and because the punishment to which they would be subject were they to refuse to work is, most of them believe, incommensurate with the conceivable political gain. Nevertheless, it must be firmly understood that by working, political prisoners are aiding and abetting the prison system. The critical question is: were they to stop working, could they thereby significantly hinder the operation of that system which holds them captive? Small in number and dispersed as they presently are in different institutions, it is our opinion that they could not. Were they to stop working it would be incorrect to assume that many—if any—nonpolitical prisoners would follow their lead. It is far more probable that other prisoners would misinterpret such an act and would view such a refusal to work as an attempt to gain special and privileged dispensations for political prisoners.

Any refusal to work, whether on an individual or group basis, is certain to lead to banishment in administrative, and in some prisons disciplinary, segregation. (Administrative and disciplinary segregation represent degrees of solitary confinement, the latter being the more complete of the two. In administrative segregation, the prisoner is afforded greater privileges regarding such things as reading matter, accommodations, showers, and sometimes food.) For as long as the inmate remains adamant and continues to refuse job assignments, his exile from the prison population will be permanent. But it should be appreciated that any prolonged isolation of a political prisoner from the general population renders him thoroughly impotent in terms of prison political life. A handful of political prisoners have assumed such a position of non-cooperation and we assure the reader that the effect of their protest upon other political prisoners as well as the general inmate population has been nonexistent.

Organized and concerted work stoppages do, of course, have a place in prison resistance. But these group actions are a far cry from individual acts of protest. In the same context, individual acts of sabotage, though easily effectuated, are of no greater than nuisance value and are, in our opinion, not worth the risk entailed.

(The following addendum is by David Miller.)

While in prison, I held five different jobs. At Allenwood I was on the general farm detail and also on a construction detail; at the penitentiary I worked in food service; at the farm camp outside the penitentiary I worked on the general farm crew as well as in the power plant. I never did any more than I had to, and always carried a book or periodical small enough to conceal so that I could take every opportunity to R&R (rest and read).

The job that I'll remember for a long time to come was at Lewisburg while on the farm crew. First, there was the cabbage patch: several of us spent weeks hoeing a couple of acres of cabbage that had gotten completely out of hand; later we harvested. We worked as slowly as possible, and sat down as soon as the detail officer drove away to check something else. Ray, an ex-marine and gifted goldbricker, Jimmy King, a brother from Newark, Jerry, a frustrated soccer player from Baltimore, and I played football with cabbages, usually kicking field goals which Jerry won. But the worst of it was the potato patch.

There were sixteen acres of potatoes. When harvested and stored in the root cellar at the rear of the penitentiary, they would last the institution for three months. The potato digger turned the earth over and laid the potatoes on the ground. We had to pick them by hand with buckets, fill 100-pound bags, and transport them to the root cellar. The whole job could have been done in less than two weeks; we worked so hard at avoiding work that we managed to stretch the job over a two-month period. It was excruciating, and incredibly boring, but we were determined. We sat down whenever the hack was out of sight; we played games: throwing a bucket high in the air and trying to hit it with potatoes before it hit the ground; we threw potatoes at one another's feet, saying, "Dance, motherfucker!" We were so slow that frost got two rows of potatoes before we got them into the cellar.

One advantage that I had on the farm crew was to tend

the little vegetable garden next to our tool- and tractor-sheds. With seeds and plants provided by a hack, we had three dozen tomato plants, a dozen bell pepper plants, two dozen hot pepper plants, a few rows of cucumbers, and some watermelon and cantaloupe hills. I watered and hoed and protected against thieves as much as possible; and I saw to it that each man got his share of the produce.

My favorite pastime during working hours—when I could manage it—was fishing. If the hack was working with a couple of inmates on a tractor or if he left us alone for a while in the farm shop, I would walk down the road 100 yards to a creek that ran adjacent to the reservation the penitentiary was on. I had a few hooks and some line that an inmate on the grounds crew found alongside the creek, and I dug worms next to the creek. I caught rock bass, sunfish, and bullheads. They were pan-size, but it would have been too much of a hassle to clean them and cook them on a hot plate back at camp. (It was a different story in the winter with the pheasants.) In the spring, the carp come up the creek to spawn, and feed close to the shore line. I speared a six-pounder—with a silage fork. On a later try I threw the silage fork too far and it still lies on the bottom of the creek.

The last job I had in prison was at the power plant just outside the penitentiary wall. I requested a transfer out of the farm crew as soon as the weather turned cold since I saw that instead of letting us sit by the pot-bellied stove in the farm shop, as he should have done, the detail officer intended to get us out in the cold to cut brush. I didn't want any part of that and asked for an indoor job. For the last four months of my sentence, I cleaned the basement of the power plant. (I don't like the look of electric floor brushes anymore.) Again, I turned a two-week into a two-month job: it was truly "make-work."

Chapter 19   WORK RELEASE

In 1965, Congress amended Title 18 of the Federal Code to include a section intended primarily for the creation of a work-release program in Federal prisons. Henceforth, inmates might be permitted to work in civilian jobs—for remuneration—in communities adjacent to each Federal prison, provided the employment of prisoners did not adversely affect the labor situation in the particular area. At present, most Federal prisons have a work-release program.

The idea behind work release is threefold. It is supposedly a rehabilitation tool that enables inmates who have a poor work record to obtain job experience under supervision; it attempts to provide the inmate with earned money to send home to his family if it is in need; it also hopes to give the inmate a small bank roll, through savings, upon his release.

Work release, however, is not available to all inmates. The first criterion in order to qualify is that a candidate must have minimum-security classification. The second is that an inmate must have less than one year left to his sentence before he can become part of the program: in some places—Allenwood for instance—an inmate is not placed in the program until he has no more than six months left to serve.

There are other criteria that narrow the field of candidates for work release. To our knowledge, no political prisoner has ever been approved; no inmate who has O.C. (Organized Crime) stamped on his jacket (record file) is allowed to participate; no inmate who has a history of violence on his record is admitted. Technically, political prisoners and organized-crime inmates *can* get work release: but it has to be approved from Washington and never is. In talks with prison administrators, political prisoners have been told that they, together with the "O.C.'s," are considered "criminals by choice" and therefore not rehabilitative; work release is not for them.

Some work-release programs are reportedly better than others, differing between institutions. The program at Allenwood is particularly poor. At Allenwood, there are, at any one time, about twenty men out of a population of 350 on work release. While in the program, these men have to pay the institution for room and board, daily transportation, and laundry; they are driven to their jobs every morning by an inmate work-release driver and picked up by him in the evening; they still live in the institution with the rest of the inmate population; there is no difference in their daily lives except that now they have jobs on the outside. Since they are earning a little cash, they are made to contribute to their upkeep. (The contributions are *not* nominal. These men hand over nearly half their earnings.)

The jobs that inmates work at are almost exclusively low-paying, menial ones. Those that we recall were work in the brick factory and sewage system, maintenance of a local golf course, and jobs of a similar nature. We cannot say for sure whether these jobs were the only ones available in the area or if only low-paying, menial jobs were looked for by those who run the program on the prison staff. We believe the latter more closely approximates the truth. (One inmate told us that he informed the man in charge of the work-release program that he could sell cars. The prison employee laughed and said that no one was sent out on that kind of job.)

The attitude of the prison staff toward work release is crystal clear to most prisoners: the staff doesn't *like* work release. Prisons have a program because they are *supposed* to have a program; if prison personnel had their way, they would probably discontinue it, preferring to keep everyone on prison territory. The staff manifests its attitude most clearly in the degree of surveillance over those inmates in the program. The turnover of work-release inmates is very high. The high rate results because of the large number of busts that the staff makes of work-release inmates. These most often occur around issues like drinking on the job, taking contraband items back to the camp, or making phone calls while at work. Because the bust rate is so high, many inmates do not even apply for work release in the first place, thinking that the risk is not worth it. There is a strong feeling that the staff is out to "get" most inmates in the program; the feeling seems pretty well founded. Inmates at Allenwood have been busted simply on suspicion of wrongdoing.

We think that there are several hidden motivations for the negative attitude of prison personnel toward work release. The first is that the prison staff does not like to work for the benefit of inmates. It takes time and energy to hunt up jobs and the prison staff is not willing to expend much of those commodities on behalf of their captives. The second is that of jealousy: staff members do not want to see any inmate make more money than they do. The third centers around the image that many prison employees like to project to the people of surrounding communities. They look upon themselves as guarding the public from hardened criminals. When inmates go out on release, work hard, and prove to be generally interesting people, the public begins to wonder about what the prison administration has been telling them all these years.

—DAVID MILLER

Chapter 20 SHORT TIME

There is a period of time toward the end of a term of imprisonment when an inmate is called a "short-timer." The term may be applied to anyone with less than ninety days to go, although sometimes a prisoner may not be greeted by his fellows with, "Hello, short-timer," until he has less than sixty days to go. But without question, if one has less than thirty days left to serve, he will think of himself by no other name than "short-timer."

The period of short time has specific problems and anxieties peculiar to it, missing or less apparent at other times. On the one hand, short time is a relief: you know that you've got them beat. The time is over. You've done the bit and you're ready to go home. Friends might say, "Well, ya got it licked, kid. This is it." Unfortunately, it is not *quite* it. There remain a month or two of imprisonment: time seems to stand still. It is quite common during these last days to develop exaggerated fears of being busted on some account, losing a lot of good time, and thereby prolonging one's imprisonment.

There also lurks in the back of the mind of a short-timer the nagging suspicion that maybe the authorities are never going to let him out! After being in prison for a few years or longer, the routine becomes so embedded as to make one think, "Was it ever any different than this?" It's hard to imagine oneself anywhere else *except* in prison: it's a chilling feeling, we guarantee.

During the last sixty days of an inmate's sentence, every institution has some sort of pre-release program. It usually consists of half-a-dozen hour-long meetings. At these meetings, films are shown on subjects like VD and safe-

driving habits. At one meeting, a parole officer is available
to answer questions about parole supervision on the street.
The pre-release program is a sham, and is hardly given
passing notice by the staff that runs it. Sometimes the person in charge of a particular meeting simply fails to
show up.

But if the prison administration does not give a damn
about the inmates, the inmates themselves should, because
readjustment to liberty after many months or years in
prison is no joke. Whether it is conscious or not, short time
causes serious anxieties about how one is going to make it
again on the outside. The most common revolve around
the pressures of earning a living and readjusting to a wife
and children. If work and family life were anywhere near
problematic before prison, they may be insurmountable
after release. The alienation that prisoners feel is clear to
many. Less clearly understood is the bitterness and alienation that occurs within an inmate's family during its struggle during the enforced separation. Both the inmate and
his family feel this, and short time—provided wife and
children are still waiting—heightens the anxieties for both.

Some men become so upset at the prospect of facing the
streets again that they seem to deliberately get into trouble
either immediately before release or shortly thereafter. Inmates like this strike us as the ostensible "successes" of the
penal system, as that system is constituted to function.
Everyone in prison is humiliated and made into dependent
beings. Those who finally become so demoralized as to
be unable to deal with their freedom for more than a few
months at a time (between bits) must make many prison
administrators and employees feel complete satisfaction at
the thought that their jobs are secure.

A personal account by one of the authors [D.M.] might
illuminate the anxieties of short time:

A little over a month before I was released, my wife and our children came to visit me at Lewisburg as they had, two or three times a month, since I had been there. The three hours' visiting time per month was usually divided into three separate visits; with two children, aged three and one, an hour in a crowded room was all they could take anyway. (Visiting is difficult at best. Catherine said that coming to the penitentiary to visit often produced in her what she called "Federal diarrhea.")

When she and our daughters arrived at 9:00 A.M. they were forced to wait until 10:30. For inmates at the farm camp, like me, the procedure runs: the officer on duty in the visiting room calls the farm camp and an officer there locates and transports the inmate to the back gate of the penitentiary. He then goes inside the penitentiary, gets an officer to take him to the visiting room, and is strip-searched before going into the visiting room. All this takes about fifteen minutes. There was no excuse for my not being called promptly; it was simply harassment. Such delays are not uncommon when inmates are out of favor with the hacks, or when visitors are those whom the hacks dislike. Catherine fell into the latter category and I into the former.

The children became restless and so did Catherine as time passed and I didn't show. She went down the hall to the warden's office to ask for me. She was upset, but asked the warden in a civilized tone the reason for the delay. He replied that he didn't know where I was and ventured that perhaps I was hiding—that I might be playing games with them. It was a tactless, ridiculous statement and Catherine became very upset. She shouted, the children cried, and Catherine cursed the warden in front of visitors and hacks.

I got to the visiting room about that time and was subsequently able to calm the situation down. Catherine and the children and I visited for a time and then they left. I was called into the associate warden's office after the visit—as I knew I would be. I had assured Catherine (and it proved true) that they would not do anything to me since I had not done anything out of line. The associate warden advised me that Catherine was to be refused permission to visit in the future. He indicated that if she made an apology, in writing, to the warden the matter might be rethought: I was to inform her of this in a letter. I wrote that evening and told her several things: that I had not been punished, that she was not going to be allowed in without an apology, that I did not think she would or that she should apologize, that I was not worried about the visiting because I had only four or five weeks to go, and that I would worry more if she came up to the penitentiary and tried to get in than if we simply forgot about visiting for the remainder of the time. Since there was no way to communicate other than by mail, I had to be frank even though I knew the letter would be read by the associate warden.

The day after I mailed the letter was February 26. (I was scheduled to be released on March 27.) While at work at the power plant that afternoon, one of the officers came to me and said that I had to go back to the dorm and pack my things, that I was going home the next day. He had gotten a call from the farm dormitory officer who, in turn, had gotten a call from someone in the penitentiary.

I was surprised and pleased—to say the least! I went back to the dorm, started shaking people's hands, then packed the things I wanted to take home. Driven to the back gate of the penitentiary with my belongings, I proceeded to the R&D (Receiving & Discharge) section. The R&D officer expected me and told the inmate workers to rush me through "dress out" because I was going home the next day. A few minutes later, in the middle of trying on a pair of pants, the R&D officer came and said that I need not rush after all: he just got a call that it was all a mistake. I was going home next month, not this one.

I went back to the farm dorm and told the story to my friends. They didn't believe it at first, but after a while they did; everyone thought that it was a pretty mean trick, and a reprisal for what Catherine had said the day before in the visiting room. Most of the inmates already knew of that incident through the fast-traveling prison "wire." I don't know whether it was reprisal or not: it's difficult in prison at times to distinguish between incompetence and baseness. But whichever it was, it did tend to make me a bit anxious during the last days. It was nothing too difficult to overcome, but the nagging suspicion that they might never let me out became a little more pronounced because of the "mistake."

Chapter 21   PAROLE

The authority to grant or deny parole rests with the United States Board of Parole in Washington, D.C. According to law, each inmate is eligible for parole upon the completion of one-third of his sentence, except in the case of the indeterminate sentence, where the inmate is eligible any time after he has served sixty days. Although the Board has the power to grant or deny parole, it in fact takes its cue from the administration at each institution. Theoretically, the institution is supposed to exert only an advisory influence on the decision but a profound influence is what it does exert; other than a five- or ten-minute personal interview with the inmate the Parole Board has nothing to go on except the inmates' written record (his "jacket")—and this is compiled by the institution.

When his parole date approaches, every inmate is entitled to a personal interview with a traveling Board member who visits thirty-odd Federal institutions every other month. Thus, during the hearing itself, the Parole Board is represented by a single member, together with the inmate's case-worker. The members all work and travel out of Washington, D.C., but for the purposes of the "personal hearings," each has a specific route mapped out for him: the man for the Eastern area might hold hearings at Allenwood and Lewisburg for a couple of weeks, then move on to Petersburg for a week, then to Atlanta, and so on.

The "personal hearing" is a ludicrous proceeding lasting, at the most, fifteen minutes. The Board member asks a wide range of questions to which he already has the answers—since they are all contained in the prisoner's "jacket" which he has before him. Within the time of the brief interview the Board member is supposed to discern what kind of "attitude" the inmate projects. The interview is tape-recorded and the inmate's case-worker sits idly by and observes the proceedings. Based on this interview, the inmate's record, and the institution's recommendations, the Parole Board makes its decision a month or two later. It is then forwarded to the institution and the case-worker informs the inmate of the good or bad news.

The supposed purpose of parole is to take an inmate out of prison and integrate him into the larger community under the special supervision of the parole authorities. Parole, it is said, is intended to be a progressive innovation that does away with the harshness of long prison terms, but still retains some of the benevolent supervision an inmate needs. In reality, though, parole serves no such function. The first real purpose of parole is behavior control within the prison. Parole is the biggest prize in the prison system's grab bag. As elusive as it may be, it serves the purpose of luring prisoners into cooperation with the authorities. It seems that no matter how far out of the question parole might be, or how overwhelmingly disheartening the chances for it are, each inmate invariably hopes against hope that *he* will obtain parole at the earliest possible date. If the date goes by, well then, it will happen the next time; and if that date goes by, it *has* to come the next time for sure—and so on.

The operation of the Federal parole system is a bit more sophisticated than simply saying "yes" or "no." In order to induce inmates to work well and cause no ripples, the Parole Board, in conjunction with local prison authorities, makes a studied use of the "set-off" and the "progress report." A set-off is the term used when an inmate is informed by the Board that his case will be brought before it again at a date some months in the future. For example, an inmate may go up for parole after a third of his sentence is served and, in turn, be told by the Parole Board that he has a twelve-month set-off; he will have another hearing one year later. (The set-off is generally employed the first time an inmate goes up for parole.) The progress report is similar to the set-off except that it usually comes after a set-off and implies that there is a better chance of making parole next time around. The so-called "special" progress report is loaded with good omens for the expectant inmate—he who has a special progress report coming up in several months is really on his toes.

The manipulative aspects of these policies become clear when, after being imprisoned for some time, one notices who makes parole and what actually constitutes "progress" in the eyes of the authorities. The best descriptive term we have heard for "progress" is what one inmate termed "humility." "Humility" means that an inmate causes the authorities no trouble; it means that the inmate accepts the dictum that he is wrong and the courts and prison authorities right. (A serious breach of humility would be for a prisoner to write a writ in protest against intolerable prison conditions.) Humility further means that an inmate cooperates to the fullest extent with the "program" worked out or suggested to him by the Classification and Parole staff; that he works well at whatever job is given him and, in fact, volunteers for difficult jobs and extra work; that he joins a number of service organizations and becomes involved in extracurricular activities. If an expectant parolee is a drug addict, he had better join Narcotics Anonymous; if an alcoholic, AA. Many a man has been told this directly by the Classification and Parole staff. Playing up to the chaplains, joining the Jaycees, volunteering for heart-research projects and other human guinea-pig experiments, partaking in group therapy sessions—all these things contribute to an inmate's parole-campaign strategy. And lastly, snitching is not to be overlooked as a means of earning early parole. Cooperation is the watchword; "humility" the underlying principle.

Even so, those inmates who cooperate to the fullest and who wear their humility on their sleeves are not assured of early parole; but enough of those who try this route do make it and thereby encourage others. However, the prison authorities are powerful enough to frustrate even their best cooperators—and still find more comers knocking at their door. In terms of recommending parole, they are ambivalent about some of their super cooperators because they do not want any others getting the wrong impression; i.e., that just any inmate can get parole by going through the motions. Optimally, a prospective parolee should be truly broken, spiritually and psychologically. The *truly* humble must therefore be separated from the sham humble.

It is not our intention to lump together into the category of the truly humble all those who belong to religious, psychotherapeutic, or service organizations. Neither do we intend to make value judgments, or criticize those inmates who follow a cooperative plan in the hope of making parole—although there *are* a number of ostentatious cooperators who are truly repulsive. The thrust of our criticism is directed against those people and that system that demand such degrading behavior in lieu of further punishment.

But if humility is what earns parole, and is what the administration likes to see, we must add that there are inmates who do not fully cooperate and yet still make parole—usually, however, toward the end of their sentences. These inmates are subject to the second function of the Federal Parole System: punishment and harassment. The authorities' use of parole as punishment is made clear when we see what a violated parolee loses, how many parolees are violated, and the reasons for such violations.

When an inmate is granted parole, he remains under the supervision of the Board of Parole in the person of his district parole officer—for the duration of his sentence. If, for instance, an inmate made parole after twenty-four months in prison on a five-year sentence, he would be on parole for thirty-six months. His parole *could* be dropped after a year or so, but he might well be on parole for the full three years. While on parole, the parolee is subject to very strict regulations regarding his living habits. He must not change his residence or his job, or travel outside his district, or marry without the consent of his parole officer; he cannot register at a hotel with a woman who is not his wife; he cannot associate with people who have criminal records. If the parole officer so decides, he can indicate certain individuals with whom the parolee is forbidden to associate—even though they may have *no* criminal record.

Most violators are returned for forbidden associations, or for traveling without permission. The Board of Parole admits that about forty per cent of those paroled return to prison as violators. A parolee can be busted for associating with known criminals even if he doesn't know that they are criminals. (A parolee can run into such people anywhere, in a bar or at a party, etc.) He can also be busted if he doesn't call his parole officer soon enough after returning from a trip—even though he had permission for the trip.

Federal courts seem to cooperate extremely well with parole authorities. The procedure for a parole bust is to have the parolee picked up by the FBI, then given a parole-violation hearing before a Federal judge. It has only been as recently as a couple of years ago that a parolee won the right to be represented by a lawyer at this hearing; but no matter anyway. The hearing is a rubber-stamp process for the parole officer. Most often, the parolee is technically "guilty" of whatever the officer alleges. The problem is that the violations are petty and arbitrarily enforced. Because the courts cooperate so well, parole busts are easy to engineer: to put a person on parole makes it easy for Federal authorities to lock him up again. If these authorities are interested in sending someone back to prison, a parole bust is very helpful: much less time, money, and energy are consumed than are with new prosecutions. Besides, there is always the chance that the government might lose a new prosecution.

But the government doesn't lose with a parole violation —the convict loses, and loses a lot. In the Federal system (unlike most state systems), parolees do not get credit for time served under supervision on the street. If an inmate makes parole after twenty-four months on a five-year bit and if he is then busted after being on parole for two years, he has to came back to the penitentiary and do *three* years—not the remaining one year. Technically—and it has happened—a parolee can violate his parole a few days before it ends and be returned to do the several years already done under supervision on the street. Furthermore, the violator not only loses the time he did on the street, he loses the good time that he may have accumulated before he made parole. Taking our example of the man who does twenty-four months before making parole: he would normally get about 120 statutory "good days" in that time; let's say that he earned another forty "good days" in prison industry, or at a farm camp. Since he made parole, those 160 good days are lost. When he returns to prison to do the rest of the five years, he will, in effect, be starting a *new* three-year bit—although he is still serving the original sentence. On the last three years of the original five, he will get 180 statutory good days, and perhaps another sixty earned good days, so that he'll be released eight months short of the full three years. But adding on the twenty-four months that he did before making parole, and the time served in prison adds up to fifty-two months. Then add to that the time done on the street before the violation. Let's say he was out one year. We see that prison time and parole-supervision time come to a grand total of sixty-four months!

If our man had remained in prison from the start, *without* parole, he would have gotten all the statutory- and earned-good time on the entire bit, and been released from prison after forty-four months. Because he made parole and was then busted, he was penalized for an additional *twenty months*.

However, it does not end even here; there is more. If an inmate does not make parole, he is released under the terms of minimum expiration (ME) or mandatory release (MR). ME means that an inmate is released with less than 180 statutory good days and earned good days combined. MR means that an inmate is released with 180 statutory good days or more and with earned good days above and beyond the 180 statutory good days. With ME, the ex-con is said not to "owe" the Feds any time. With MR, the person owes "x" amount of time under temporary parole supervision. The time that the MR releasee owes is the good time he has earned, beyond the last 180 statutory good days of his sentence. In other words, he is under the authority of the parole board for ten months—even though *denied* parole while in prison. While under this temporary supervision, he is subject to the parole authorities in every way, just as if he had made parole; he can be busted as a parole violator in the same way. The authors have met several inmates who have been busted while on MR. It is far from uncommon.

POLITICAL PRISONERS AND PAROLE

During the two years or so that the authors were imprisoned, the general trend was for the prison authorities to want draft resisters and other war resisters to do about two years in the pokey. For example, if one had a sentence of two years, he could expect to do it all, with virtually no chance of parole. But if one had a sentence of from four to five years, and was not continually in trouble in jail, he would probably make parole by the end of twenty-four months' imprisonment.

The Youth Act sentence, or the "zip six" as it is called, is an indeterminate sentence ranging from sixty days to six years. A young man with this sentence is eligible for parole any time after sixty days and, in fact, will go before the Parole Board in less than ninety days after beginning his sentence. But the Youth Act is a trick bag, because an inmate with this sentence does not earn any extra good time whatever, and can be kept in for four years—after which time he must be turned loose. As if that is not enough, anyone who does four years under a zip six still has to do two years on parole. However it turns out, the recipient of a zip six will either be in prison or on parole for six years—whether he gets out in sixty days or four years. For the zip six, as well as for the straight sentences of up to a pound (five years), the trend has been roughly twenty-two to twenty-four months before parole.

There are, however, some exceptions. For example, JW's do less time than do most other draft resisters: they usually make parole after eighteen months' imprisonment. The reason is fairly easily explained because of their apolitical stance and high level of cooperation with the prison program. The Muslims, on the other hand, can expect to do about twenty-four months, just as other political prisoners.

Political prisoners are hardly immune from the unending conjecture that surrounds the chances of making or not making parole. We chime in with everyone else. "So and so heard back and got such and such a set-off." "Someone got a date for such and such a time. How many months will that give him?" "When do you go up again?"— and so on. Given the circumstances, it seems unavoidable that political prisoners talk about parole both among themselves and with other inmates, but they must caution themselves against falling prey to the prison administrators' game, harboring unreasonable hopes, and so becoming preoccupied with the matter. One false notion that we can dispel here and now is the idea that a political prisoner will be paroled if he causes sufficient trouble for prison officials. He will soon discover that even though the latter view him as a "troublemaker," they become rather attached to him in spite of the difficulties he may create, and he will be invited to remain with them some time, perhaps even to the expiration of his sentence.

Some of the incidents surrounding parole can only be termed Kafkaesque. A personal incident concerning one of the authors [D.M.] at his parole hearing is one. He went to the hearing and was there greeted by the Parole Board member and the case-worker. The Board member said, in essence: "Now, Mr. Miller, you have applied for a parole hearing and you are being given one because that is your right. But I see here by your record that you have forfeited some statutory good time as the result of disciplinary action. There is a Parole Board rule that anyone who has forfeited good time is not eligible for parole: that means that you can't be given parole. But go ahead and say anything you want in your behalf, and the Board will take it into consideration."

Another story is precise in spirit if not in letter. A man

at Atlanta was serving a life sentence with no recommendation for parole, followed consecutively by a twenty-five-year sentence with no recommendation for parole, followed by a fifteen-year sentence with no recommendation for parole. Prison officials wondered why the inmate was ready to kill his case-worker when the latter called him in and said, "Now, about this progress report that you got coming up."

The parole system *must* be drastically changed. An immediate change would be to make parole a right rather than a privilege. As it stands now, parole is a repressive behavior tool—that tool must be taken out of the hands of parole and prison officials. An inmate should make parole after serving one-third of his sentence unless it can be proved, *by due process,* that he has done something dastardly enough not to deserve it. The demand to make parole a protected right is one of the most important elements of prison resistance.

Reforming the street-supervision system so that each day under supervision is taken off the sentence is basic. Drastically limiting the authority of the parole officer and easing the laws concerning parole violation are the final basic demands that must be met in order to change the parole system.

One last word. We are not aware of paroled political prisoners being considered violators because of political reasons. However, the experience of Eldridge Cleaver with the California State Penal System should be viewed with some degree of alarm, since it may be but a first manifestation of what to expect from Federal authorities when the heat is really on. We have already seen that the parole system is manipulative: there is absolutely no reason to doubt that it will be used to manipulate the political lives of ex-political prisoners. The government may be

expected to use any and all means in order to quell meaningful radical activity. If it is true that *all* political activists are potential targets of repression, certainly the ex-
political con on parole would seem to be a sitting duck.

Chapter 22 SUGGESTIONS FOR REFORM

The abject failure of the American penal system in either rehabilitating or deterring criminals is so well known as to require no exhaustive reiteration. It is our feeling that the facts clearly lead to the conclusion that prisons, as they are presently structured, have no socially redeeming value and ought, in their present form, to be abolished.

The prisoner is unknown: his true life and destiny have never been made manifest before the public. The image of the prisoner that the public is allowed to glimpse is a false one and thus evokes no move to relieve his plight. Rather, society vindictively demands that the screw be given another turn. So long as the public is in need of what seems to be mass psychotherapy in the sending of men to prison, no substantial change in the penal system can be expected. A society which has not found the courage and the means to break its own shackles is in no position to break those it has placed upon its "deviant" members. Reform is not really an adequate solution. However, to do nothing but stand by and nurture a sense of futility while masses of imprisoned men, women, and even children suffer unspeakable degradation, strikes us as unconscionable. It is in this spirit that we offer the following proposals for the implementation of a prison-reform movement.

In the absence of a political and social revolution in this nation it seems apparent to us that prisoners—like unionists and suffragettes before them—will either win their own rights or sink deeper into the mud of the penal system. Sad as it is to admit, up until now the efforts of political prisoners to wage a prison-resistance movement

have been to little avail. Part of the problem is the sheer
enormity of the task; but another difficulty has been the
minuscle support that prisoners have received from outside communities. As we have noted, prison resisters incur
continuous, unremitting, and harsh retribution at the
hands of their captors. This cannot be completely elimi-
nated; however, it can be minimized to an appreciable
extent if greater cooperation and concern were forthcoming from the free community. Such support can serve as a
buffer between prisoners and officials. What can the community offer?

1. Prisoners need legal assistance. Any number of acts
of resistance in prison have come to naught because counsel could not be obtained to further them. Prison officials work most comfortably in the dark, well hidden from
public and judicial scrutiny. A mammoth blow could be
struck against this "closed society" through the interces-
sion of radically conscious attorneys. Several political prisoners have been rescued from rather difficult conditions
by the timely intervention of their lawyers. One or two
such prisoner victories predispose officials to exert greater
caution the next time. This sort of thing, in essence, "frees"
the resister so that he may resist all the more effectively.
But much more needs to be done; lawyers have only rarely
been available.

It seems to us that certain prison regulations are literally crying out for investigation by judicial intervention.
Immediate priorities for court challenges should include
prison regulations pertaining to book-and-periodical censorship—especially when it is politically inspired; the arbitrary transfer of alleged "agitators" from prison to prison;
and the autocratic revocation of good time at the whim
and fancy of the chief warden.

We do not anticipate that prisoners in general—or political prisoners in particular—can rely exclusively on judicial intervention in their struggle against the Federal Bureau of Prisons. Nonetheless, legal assistance is sorely needed; its absence dooms prison resistance from the outset.

2. Political prisoners and nonpolitical prisoners are greatly in need of an inmate "service center": such a center's goals would be manifold, a primary one being to establish lines of communication with prisoners and the outside world. The center could arrange to send books to prisoners; it could purchase gift subscriptions to various publications in the name of specific prisoners and provide correspondents for those who may have a need for the same; it could arrange periodic visits to prisoners, and publish information about them and the specific prison conditions they live with and the treatment they are receiving. The center would also offer counseling services for prisoners and their families.

It is to be hoped that the center might eventually establish small chapters in the various towns and cities in which the larger prisons are located. In this way, the immediate needs of the prisoners could be better served at the local level; local community support for them could be generated. While many prisons are located in desolate, out-of-the-way locations where wide community support cannot be anticipated, others are within major cities or close to university towns where such support might be expected. Finally, the service center might consider raising funds to support "houses of hospitality" (see "Visiting"), in order to aid dependents of prisoners and provide commissary money for inmates without funds.

We have stressed that prisoners must lead their own struggle; however, political organizing within the prisons will remain ineffective until outside support is clearly in evidence. Nonpolitical prisoners feel isolated and, in fact, are. They cannot be expected to join political prisoners until we can assure them that ours is not a will-o'-the-wisp protest but a group solidly backed by organizations with access to the courts and the mass media.

3. Finally, there is a need for highly visible mass demonstrations—of all varieties—outside of prisons, initiated upon requests of prisoners. Protests before prisons would immediately have a twofold effect: first, the morale of political prisoners would be bolstered; second, the stock nonpolitical prisoners place in their political counterparts would be strengthened. Ultimately, such demonstrations would publicize specific prison problems and abuses and destroy the anonymity in which prison bureaucrats operate.

In certain localities such protests could have a more specific focus. For example, in those prisons located near universities and colleges, students and faculty members might demand that their schools offer full scholarships to all minimum-security prisoners who wish to avail themselves of college studies. Prisoners, in such situations, might be welcomed on campus and an effort could thus be initiated to "break down" the thirty-foot-high prison walls. Likewise, there is no rational reason why high-school remedial courses should not be taught prisoners by college students on the college campus or adjacent sites.

Where law schools exist close to a prison, law students could be encouraged to offer their assistance to all prisoners who wish to file writs on their own behalf.

Where prisons are located within or near industrial centers, good-paying jobs should be demanded for inmates. Once again, the thrust of the demand is an insistence that prison walls should, to as great an extent as possible, be "torn down."

In conclusion, we offer a list of demands that we feel provides a focus and direction for a prison-resistance movement.

They are:

1. Monthly visiting furloughs.
2. Conjugal visits with no restrictions as to who may be the partner.
3. Democratically elected inmate councils with unrestricted access to the news media.
4. A Federal minimum wage for all inmates and an end to involuntary servitude.
5. Due-process rights in good-time forfeiture board hearings.
6. Parole as a right rather than a privilege, with due-process rights included.
7. An end to censorship of mail, books and periodicals, prison manuscripts, and prison newspapers.
8. No punishment for private, consenting homosexual relations.
9. An end to arbitrary transfers; due-process procedures prior to any transfer.
10. Realistic vocational-training programs, and greatly expanded use of work release and study release, as well as guaranteed employment with state and Federal governments after release.
11. Full access, upon prisoner's request, to any doctor, clergyman, journalist, lawyer, or law student.

We would wish to live eventually in a society that did not find it necessary to imprison human beings. To this end we will continue to struggle to help create a society where, as Peter Maurin said, "'it is easier for men to be good." The struggle is, we believe, in progress.